rooted

CREATING A SENSE OF PLACE

CONTEMPORARY STUDIO FURNITURE

THE FURNITURE SOCIETY

Steffanie Dotson & Douglas Congdon-Martin, EDITORS

Schiffer Publishing Ltd®

4880 Lower Valley Road • Atglen, PA 19310

Other Schiffer Books on Related Subjects:
Mind & Hand: Contemporary Studio Furniture, 2012 by The Furniture Society.
ISBN: 978-0-7643-4115-1

Copyright © 2015 by The Furniture Society

Library of Congress Control Number: 2015936794

Designed by Justin Watkinson
Type set in Univers LT Std

ISBN: 978-0-7643-4948-5
Printed in China

Published by Schiffer Publishing, Ltd.
4880 Lower Valley Road
Atglen, PA 19310
Phone: (610) 593-1777; Fax: (610) 593-2002
E-mail: Info@schifferbooks.com

For our complete selection of fine books on this and related subjects, please visit our website at www.schifferbooks.com. You may also write for a free catalog.

This book may be purchased from the publisher. Please try your bookstore first.

We are always looking for people to write books on new and related subjects. If you have an idea for a book, please contact us at proposals@schifferbooks.com.

Schiffer Publishing's titles are available at special discounts for bulk purchases for sales promotions or premiums. Special editions, including personalized covers, corporate imprints, and excerpts can be created in large quantities for special needs. For more information, contact the publisher.

contents

preface

This book began as a visual glimpse into the furniture exhibited as part of The Furniture Society annual conference, FS14 – Rooted: Creating a Sense of Place, which convened in Port Townsend, Washington, June 18–22, 2014. The conference was hosted by the Port Townsend School of Woodworking, whose mission is to inspire a life-long passion for craftsmanship through education in woodworking and traditional crafts. The school sits within Fort Worden State Park at the tip of the Olympic Peninsula in the Pacific Northwest. The location is not only beautiful, but a place where boat building, navigating, and sailing are rooted deep in the hearts of the locals. In fact, just down the road, the Northwest School of Wooden Boatbuilding teaches and preserves traditional and contemporary boatbuilding skills. In conjunction with FS14, an offsite exhibition was hosted at the Northwest Woodworkers' Gallery in Seattle, Washington. The exhibition, titled *A Sense of Place*, was curated by Furniture Society member Peter Pierobon, NWG Director Sharon Ricci, and Port Townsend School of Woodworking Executive Director Tim Lawson. It was a pleasure to draw together so many respectable institutions in the name of furniture.

The following pages contain many images of Furniture Society members' work. We owe thanks to the folks who made submissions and shared statements about it. The scope of the book expanded midway through the project to allow all Furniture Society members to submit work for inclusion. So, in addition to the work exhibited at FS14, members who were not able to attend the conference or exhibit work there are also included within these pages. Giving us more than just a visual glimpse, the addition of an artist statement from each maker offers access to the maker's mind, creating a truer connection while viewing the work. I enjoyed reading each one during the editing process.

STEFFANIE DOTSON

Accompanying the images are excerpts from conference presentations and essays written around the conference theme, "Rooted: Creating A Sense of Place." We have also to thank the authors who contributed essays.

All images and essays were generously contributed to this publication without compensation to the maker or author, and for that, I would like to sincerely thank each and every person for their generosity.

Thanks also to Schiffer Publishing for producing a beautiful book and believing in The Furniture Society and its members.

When we expanded the scope of the book to include members outside the conference, we expanded the essence of *Rooted* and created a broader sense of place allowing the contribution of more members. Some of the images you'll see in *Rooted* may not register to every reader as furniture. As an organization mainly comprised of craftspeople who genuinely seek pleasure in working to create beautiful objects, we welcome the blending of furniture, objects, and materials—a different perspective helps break boundaries and prevent stagnation. Although the lines may be blurred now and then, The Furniture Society is, in a word, a community, where creative makers share their insights, talents, designs, and enthusiasm for their craft.

Steffanie Dotson
President
The Furniture Society Board of Trustees

Bebe and Warren Johnson: 2014 Award of Distinction Honorees

The dynamic duo being recognized with this year's Furniture Society Award of Distinction is the imitable Bebe Pritam Johnson and Warren Eames Johnson. I think it is safe to say that without Bebe and Warren it is unlikely that there would be a Furniture Society as we know it. I know I would have never been on the radar without Bebe's encouragement. I owe her a great deal.

Most of us know Bebe and Warren as the thoughtful, careful, and intentional owners of Pritam & Eames, the nation's premier gallery for Studio Furniture. One wonders, however, what brought them to this point.

Warren and Bebe both studied philosophy early in their academic careers. After receiving her master's degree in communications from Boston University, Bebe would begin her real-world career and become the director of Asian Program Operations at the Council on International Educational Exchange in New York. Warren studied law and received an LLB from the University of Illinois, and pursued graduate economics at MIT. His career took a turn, however, when the Johnsons moved to New York, and he ended up studying film at Columbia University where he received an MFA. Warren co-authored a book on film production, taught film at various institutions including Columbia, and was cameraman/editor on a number of internationally based documentaries. After an interesting and successful decade, Warren and Bebe decided it was time for a change.

So, following the likes of De Kooning, Pollack, and Larsen, they decamped to East Hampton, a bit before the glitterati of the 1980s and 1990s and, in another turn of career, carved out a life dedicated to craft: educating and offering to the public a retail opportunity, a public that sought them out in a historic old laundry building in East Hampton that became Pritam & Eames. For the last 33 years, Pritam & Eames has existed, both powerfully and quietly, out in Long Island for a very appreciative public.

Bebe and Warren were not satisfied with just selling the best studio furniture, they were also ambitious to contribute to the growing body of literature about this decorative arts field. This ambition led to conversations with makers and other intelligent aficionados that resulted in the publication of their book, *Speaking of Furniture: Conversations with 14 American Masters* [The Artist Book Foundation, 2013].

Personally, I can't imagine anyone more deserving of the Award of Distinction than Bebe Pritam Johnson and Warren Eames Johnson. They built and crafted a business that has sustained them, given a boost to grateful makers, and played an important part in building the dialogue that underpins today's studio furniture movement.

Notes from Andrew Glasgow, past executive director of The Furniture Society and the American Craft Council, about this year's honorees.

ANDREW GLASGOW

reconnecting the craftsman with the community

TIM LAWSON

Local craftsmen and local materials have been at the heart of furniture making for most of its existence. With exploration of the globe came access to new materials, new techniques, and new inspiration.

The wheel has turned—focus is returning to local resources. The local food movement has a powerful call—connecting the consumer with the farmer next door. As furniture makers we need to accept the local challenge and reconnect the consumer with craftsmen in their community and local sources of materials.

Every region has a distinct voice—climate and topography govern the woods available, history drives the narrative, each region has a palette of colors, and local industries produce other materials. How do our creations reflect our history, communities, and surroundings?

We'd like to challenge the current generation of makers to think about the local narratives and styles that we will pass on to future generations of makers. Can we create the dialog, styles, and visions that will be the foundation for the future?

Tim Lawson is the founder and executive director of the Port Townsend School of Woodworking. He and his team served as the gracious hosts of FS14.

reflecting on place, material, and technology

PERRY PRICE

First, a confession.

During the annual member's meeting on Saturday morning of The Furniture Society conference, I went to the beach. Launching into the waters of Port Townsend Bay from the sand that morning were dozens of boats intent on rowing the sound to nearby Rat Island and back for the 20th annual Rat Island Regatta. Among the various vessels was a handful of racing shells, built by legendary Seattle builders George Pocock and his son, Stan. The elite racing boats of their day and used by university and Olympic teams across the country, lovingly restored and maintained by the local club, the needle-thin cedar vessels continued to be rowed by crews of four or eight when countless more sit idle, forgotten or unrepaired. The boats, with their cedar glowing under clear layers of varnish against the mild swell of the water, were an ephemeral interjection to the proceedings of the conference on the hill at Fort Worden State Park— FS14 Rooted: Creating a Sense of Place.

A sense of place does not require a large leap of imagination for the craftsperson. After all, those individuals devoted to the investigation and manipulation of material in the production of unique objects are grounded in a notion of the physical—from the source of the material to the physical space the object inhabits on completion, and all of the little conceptions of space in between. A potter may be removed from the digging and refining of the clay they employ, just as a furniture maker may select wood harvested across the globe, yet neither can easily ignore the material characteristics that render it unique. The variety in texture and plasticity that different clay bodies present or the behavior of a particular species of wood are unavoidable, characteristics developed and affected by the locale of their origins. Place is as much a physical quality of material as color, texture, or composition.

Place as physical quality has suffered in our contemporary era, an age in which the manufacture of the lion's share of our everyday material culture is completed beyond a distant horizon and formed of materials compiled and synthesized from somewhere else. A correction to the state of affairs has been felt most acutely around our sources of food, driven first by the consumer whose general malaise around quality, health, and safety is followed, in turn, by increased demand for local quality food that cuts across demographics. Our material culture has seen only limited comparable success. The few examples typically feature fiber and ceramics, the production of modest and relatively disposable objects rather than the durable goods of the heirloom quality usual of studio and artisan furniture. That the furniture of the caliber we celebrate is most typically bespoke— that is, produced to the specifications of the artist, the client, or both and in limited quantities—challenges any direct comparison.

But the dissatisfaction with available goods is not unique to our source of food nor is it particularly new. Nearly fifty years ago, Hedy Backlin argued, in her piece "Education for Design" for *Craft Horizons,* that poor industrial design resulted from an adherence to the lowest common denominator and saw the craftsperson as the antidote. The maker, she wrote, "is alert and responsive to [a material's] inherent aesthetic and technical possibilities." Craftspeople had ignored an opportunity to design for industry as an enriching alternative—fiscally and artistically— to the limitations of the studio or an academic appointment. The barrier, Backlin argued, was craft artists' limited understanding of the processes involved in industrial fabrication. Few could translate effectively their handmade work into instruction for the production line. The Bauhaus, the German art school founded in 1919 that espoused a synthesis of form and material, ideas, and implantation, seemed a ready-fit to produce the designer/craftsman Backlin wished to see. "Architects, sculptors, painters, we all must return to the crafts" read the 1919 Bauhaus manifesto. The school's instructors were divided among masters of form and masters of craft, the former teaching color, line, and composition, the latter what was needed to ensure the thing didn't fall apart. But the school was closed by the National Socialist Party in 1933 and its influential faculty and graduates were dispersed across Europe and the United States. Only echoes of the Bauhaus pedagogy can be found now in the many craft programs and schools here at home.

Backlin's industrial design-fluent craftsman might address a material dissatisfaction with manufactured products, but it does not follow that such items would convey a sense of place. The international style promoted by the Bauhaus was driven more by the use of industrial materials and processes, such as chairs designed to employ standard metal tubing to streamline manufacture. The architecture of The Miller Hull Partnership, presented at the *Rooted* conference by partner Craig Curtis, emphasizes sustainability and use of local materials, but in form owes more to the long shadow of the international style of architecture and the energy crisis of 1973 than to any regional vernacular of the Pacific Northwest.

The perseverance and tenacity of vernacular forms are not immediately clear. Technologies, both the rapidly evolving and the stubbornly fixed featured at the *Rooted* conference, offer few answers. Both technologies featured prominently in the complex nexus of lectures, meetings, demonstrations, and workshops. Equally captivating were demonstrations on the use of Japanese hand planes by Tak Yoshino or traditional Northwest carving techniques using bent knives and various adzes by David Franklin, as the digiFabulous event offered ShopBot CNC machines working away under the direction of Ted Hall, Reuben Foat, Kimo Griggs, and Christy Oates. Yet despite appearances, that the former would be tied to specific means of vernacular fabrication while the latter seemingly unencumbered by specificity of the local, neither set of tools can be assumed to assert or deny a sense of place by their use or misuse. More challenging, particularly around digitally aided fabrication, was any consensus on the effects of their implementation. Still questionable is whether or not the means of digitally aided fabrication is currently utilized in a manner that is unique and unreproducible by other means—no matter how onerous those non-digital means might be. And, allowing the previous estimation that place be considered a physical quality of the material, can we say the same for the very code used in digital fabrication? Do we afford to the tool and the process the same interpretation and critical analysis as the material?

Yet perhaps the distance between the restored Pocock cedar rowing shells in Port Townsend Bay and recent digitally aided fabrication is not so vast. Christy Oates's E-waste Project of 2011 is a reflection of a less than picturesque location, a San Diego electronic waste recycling center, and a virtual, non-location, the aptly named web that digitally ties our world together through the personal technology of our daily life. The visual details of the now obsolete and broken circuits may be abstracted, rendered digitally, and laser-cut by machine, yet the work remains a document of its time and means of fabrication. Our new vernacular may reside in the intersection of the virtual and the physical, with work and techniques, such as these, as landmarks and signifiers of our progress forward.

Perry is the director of education for the American Craft Council, where he is responsible for programming and outreach providing thought leadership and cultivating critical thinking on the field of contemporary craft. Prior to joining the ACC, he served as Curator of Exhibitions and Collections for Fuller Craft Museum in Brockton, Massachusetts. He is a graduate of the Cooperstown Graduate Program in Museum Studies and Johns Hopkins University, and is a scholar of American craft, design, and material culture.

rooted

PETER PIEROBON

I would like to start this discussion on *Rooted—Creating a Sense of Place* by acknowledging the fourteenth Furniture Society conference. I remember, back in 1996, being part of a small group that became the steering committee that met several times in Philadelphia and flushed out the structure and future for the Society. I don't think that any of us at the time could have predicted how the Society would unfold and how strong it would be after seventeen years of existence.

Each year the conference moves to a new location and engages a different group of participants. This is part of the beauty of this organization, as, in turn, each geographical area gets to share its history, its celebrities, and its future with the rest of us. Furniture, as you all know, is not easily transported and so we focus our attention on the local makers, materials, and history, and this dovetails perfectly with the theme of this year's conference. It also becomes obvious, as time goes by, that we are all part of a larger continuum, and each of us adds to the history of our field and affects its course and direction while nurturing new roots.

There are many kinds of roots, of course. But the obvious example for us furniture folks is the tree and its structural roots that provide stability, nutrients, and water. Roots primarily remain hidden, doing their work out of sight, but are never forgotten. And their job is helped by the relationship of millions of microbes that live in the soil and break down or change certain nutrients that allow the plants to take up these nutrients successfully. As many things in nature are, this turns out to be a carefully balanced, interdependent relationship that is very complex and fragile. Additionally, there are the roots we all create that attach us to each other and to the place that we live. These roots take time to develop, but, once formed, are often life-long and provide a way forward through the many changes in life.

When I think of furniture and how it is able to express the thoughts and feelings of a community, I immediately think of the Shakers. Has any other movement been able to capture and share the commitment and devotion of an entire group so successfully? They produced spare, unadorned, utilitarian pieces that were light in weight and built with integrity. To this day, their designs are as popular as ever and originals are highly collected because they embody an ideal that can be admired and appreciated no matter what the current design trends are.

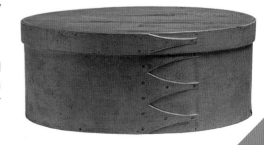

There is an authenticity to their work, a simple honesty and utility. This is a perfect example of how furniture design can embody the character and philosophy of its community. I don't believe that it is possible in this modern world, with instant communication and access to all materials, that one movement can encapsulate an entire society's beliefs, but on an individual basis there is a lot that can be done. To illustrate this, I will use my own work and life journey to share one possible outcome of what can, and in my case, did happen.

It is somewhat ironic that I am giving this speech on "Rooted," as, in order to become that, I have been one of the most active vagabonds out there. Although I am now safely back on my home turf, there was a period of twenty years where I lived away in pursuit of my dreams. It all started with an amazing ten-month journey in a VW Westphalia in 1980 scouting out various options for schooling. I settled on the Wendell Castle school in Scottsville, New York. Just so you know how green I was at the time, I had travelled to Rochester, New York, to present my portfolio to Bill Keyser at the Rochester Institute of Technology and, afterwards, he suggested that I also drop in on Wendell Castle just down the road in Scottsville. I literally thought he meant there was a castle named Wendell and somehow it was worth my while to see it! What I found there, however, was amazing and a dream come true. Not a castle at all, but an old bean mill that Wendell and his wife Nancy used to live in, which had been converted into a school. As I walked in for the first time that autumn, I saw twelve students hand-planing boards at their benches in front of a roaring fire. The fire itself was burning in a handmade, sculptural, ceramic fireplace twelve feet high. Talk about ambiance! I was instantly smitten and instantly rooted.

The next four years went by quickly and, after my two years of schooling was over, Wendell hired me to work in his studio and I stayed for an additional two years. I always considered this time to be my graduate study period. Wendell is famous for completely changing his design focus at times and during my tenure there we were building a series of lavish clocks using the most exotic and expensive materials and processes possible. So, the roots I gathered there were the foundation skills necessary to make anything, but also the attitude that everything was possible and creativity was the equal of making. I watched Wendell design and I observed how he looked close and hard around himself, how he was constantly adding to his palette and willing to consider everything as a possible inspiration.

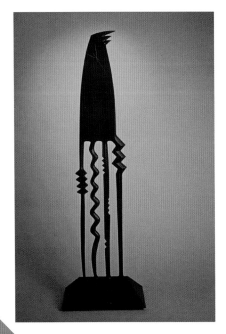

In his book *Passage to Juneau, A Sea and Its Meanings*, author Jonathon Raban observes how on very calm days, first thing in the morning, when the sea is like a mirror, the shoreline rocks are reflected back in the water perfectly and this creates a symmetrical composition that looks a lot like the totem poles carved by the indigenous first nations people. Is this a coincidence or is it a subtle, unconscious design force that worked on the locals until it appeared in their work? No one will ever know, but I believe it is possible to be influenced by your surroundings even if you are not actively seeking inspiration. The topography, weather, and materials all exert an influence in often unknown ways that can eventually show up in your work. So, therefore, I suggest that we pay attention and use all of our senses to be as aware as possible of what is around us.

I actually planned my job with Wendell to end after two years, as I knew that, if I wanted to get on with my own career, I would have to leave so it could happen. So, being a Canadian, I headed to Toronto, our largest and most affluent city, to set up my first studio. During this time I was designing and building primarily veneered, planar compositions, and was struggling to find a personal vocabulary of form. Toronto was a new city to me. I literally knew no one when I arrived there, but reached out and, as I have discovered in all of the places that I eventually lived, the community was open, kind, and welcoming. I stayed in Toronto for a little over two years; during this time, I worked hard on community building and creating friendships that have lasted to this day. My work evolved and became more urban, I started to ebonize everything, as I became more focused on the form than the material, and I often found that wood grain had a distracting effect in many circumstances. The preciousness of the material was being overtaken by the concept of the object. Also, unlike sleepy Scottsville, Toronto was a large urban city, full of galleries and museums. It was there that I discovered art indigenous to Africa, Oceania, and Australia. What spoke to me in this work was the raw, intense emotionality of the object. Often crudely made but possessing a spiritual power that few modern objects could match, it had an authenticity not unlike the Shaker's work I mentioned previously. A whole new body of work evolved as I studied and researched this new world.

In the meantime things were heating up in the gallery world. New spaces were opening and opportunities to exhibit increased. Unfortunately for me, they were all in the U.S., so, when I was offered a teaching position at the Philadelphia College of the Arts, I decided to accept and take the next step. The roots of my

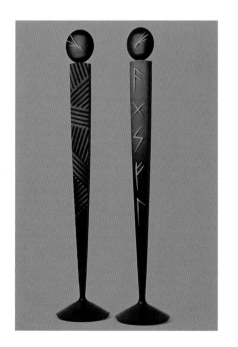
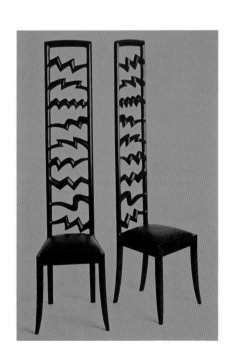
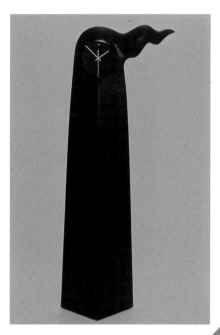

time in Toronto endure to this day; the most lasting of all would be the friendships made and the new awareness and understanding of indigenous art from around the world, which still is a primary influence in my work.

So I moved on, from one big city to another, Toronto's relative cleanliness and order was immediately apparent in contrast to the dirty, smelly craziness of Philadelphia. Teaching was a new role for me and one that I took to and enjoyed from the start. Teaching reshapes you and makes you aware of not just the information you need to share, but how to deliver it in a way that makes sense to the students as well. Teaching is expansive, inspiring, frustrating, and rewarding. I have a family of past students out in the world and keep in touch with many of them.

I spent twelve years living in Philadelphia. It was in the thick of the gallery scene on the East Coast, and I thrived emotionally and financially. My work evolved further and, as my mentor before me, I seemed to be constantly drawn to new ideas, new directions, and new opportunities. It was possible then to create an exhibition of a dozen large pieces and sell them all, with commissions as well. For me this time allowed for great experimentation and I used all sorts of materials, like cast bronze, stone, and paint, and used new processes, like welding. I increased my studies of indigenous art and started to apply surface decoration for the first time, including carving, painting, and drawing, with lots of experimenting. However, I wanted the work to be more than just decorative. I strove to add literal meaning to the decoration and started to experiment with glyphs and other sorts of decipherable markings. Hobo scratchings, musical notation, sign language, Nordic Runes, and especially Gregg shorthand became my vocabulary. It was possible to make the work very personal as a result and I often worked with clients to encode pieces with special meaning and content. An example of this is a desk I made for Stephen King, which contained three secret compartments and carries glyphs on the top saying, "All things serve the Beam." I don't know what that means to him; I figured if he wanted to share he would have done so.

Philadelphia was a tough town to live in. Break-ins were common, personal safety a daily issue... and did I mention the heat? The summers killed me. In spite of the amazing community and friends I had there, I started to think about leaving. What would I leave behind? Most of my friends were like me—in the

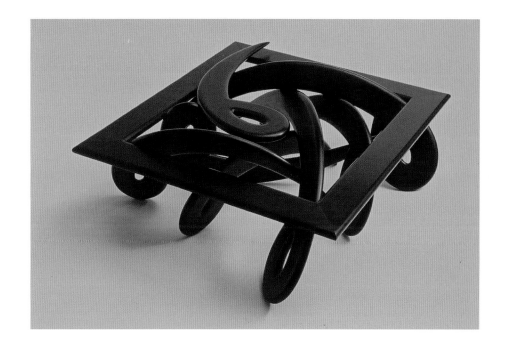

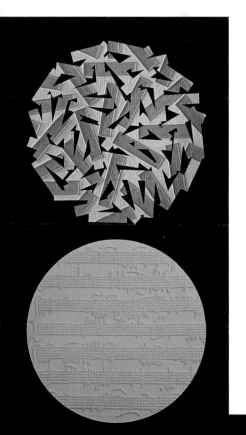

arts, transplanted from another place, no children. My students were now out in the world creating families and new businesses, but usually living somewhere else. Looking back on it, I think that twelve years of living in Philadelphia gave me the confidence to trust myself, the knowledge that I was a part of a larger community, and the courage to take risks. Teaching gave me so much—an extended family, communication skills, and new roots—that I did not know even existed before. The faculty I was a part of shaped and engaged the community and there was a real life in Philadelphia at that time in the craft community.

But, then it was time to pull up those roots once again and move on...

My next move was back to the West Coast and a new teaching position at the California College of Craft and Design, now known as the California College of Art. This program was quite different from the University of the Arts and reflected recent changes in the field that skewed more to the design world, away from the self-build, craft model I was familiar with. I only spent two years living in San Francisco and it was a turbulent time for me personally. Despite the fact that it is a large urban center, nature is not that far away from downtown San Francisco and I started to spend more time outside. The weather was fabulous and I found a great, shared studio space on an old navy yard in Oakland. Slowly but surely, this reality started to have an influence on my work. Things lightened up, natural wood reappeared for the first time in years, and a looser and more

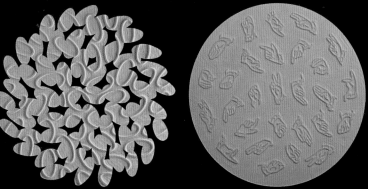

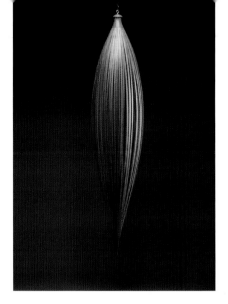

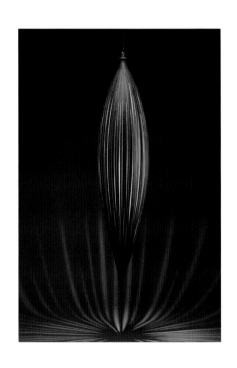

informal aesthetic evolved. I started using color seriously for the first time and left tool marks on the surfaces of the work—what liberation from the tedium of sanding! I produced several bodies of work there that emphasized the sculptural potential of my work and gave me great artistic satisfaction. Because I was now shipping work back to the East coast, I made smaller, faster work and much of it was lathe-based and sculptural.

For a variety of personal reasons, the millennium became a pivotal, transitional time for me and I decided to strike out on a year of walkabout. It was an amazing time that culminated in a return to life where it all began for me in Vancouver, Canada. Suddenly, years of inner city urban life were lifted, revealing a beautiful environment that I had forgotten about. Imagine a city where mountains rise out of the sea forming a natural backdrop covered in forests of trees. I started snowboarding, sailing, and hiking. All the activities with which I had grown up were suddenly back in my life. I started gardening and building boats, and, true to form, all of these activities have influenced my work and added to my aesthetic since my return.

For example, I built a cedar strip canoe that led directly to the creation of a series of pendant lights. Built both for the outdoors and indoors, these lights are made of many strips of wood bent around a form that allows them to hold their shape. And the shape itself is influenced by the material; just like boats, there is a fairness to the curves that speaks to vessels that must move through water. This reintroduction of marine vessels has had a profound effect on me and I have actually joined a small boat-building club to further my understanding of the various techniques of design and construction.

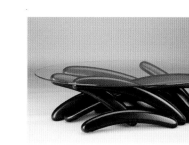

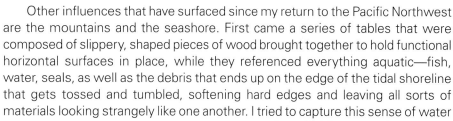

Other influences that have surfaced since my return to the Pacific Northwest are the mountains and the seashore. First came a series of tables that were composed of slippery, shaped pieces of wood brought together to hold functional horizontal surfaces in place, while they referenced everything aquatic—fish, water, seals, as well as the debris that ends up on the edge of the tidal shoreline that gets tossed and tumbled, softening hard edges and leaving all sorts of materials looking strangely like one another. I tried to capture this sense of water moving, tidal forces at play, and the effects of wind and water in my work.

After a time I shifted my focus to the mountains and went down to the local landscape supply yard looking for inspiration. I returned with a bunch of rocks and started to build pieces using the rocks as an integral part of the object. I developed some new methods of joining different materials together and particularly enjoyed the contrast of wood and stone together, natural materials collected from the local environment that express that environment in their composition.

Most recently I have become interested in plants and gardening. This has led me to explore some new

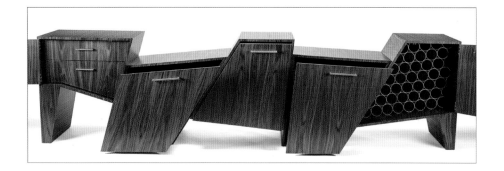

botanical compositions. The creative journey continues. As a metaphor, there is no better way to illustrate the concept of rooting than building objects inspired by nature.

In conclusion, I would like to believe that the mere fact that I have shared my thoughts and experiences with you has begun the process of knitting us together. Those little roots have begun to grow as we share our common interests and passions. Furniture can be a very personal and expressive medium; it has been my goal from the beginning to explore this opportunity. Furniture provides the foundation upon which we live our lives. It embodies our physical state and shares with us legs, arms, seats, and backs. Furniture is like the Fred Astaire and Ginger Rogers pairing; he was an amazing dancer, but she did everything he did in high heels and backwards. So respect your furniture and treat it lovingly.

My final piece illustrates this relationship we have with furniture and each other. Interdependent, supportive, emotional—the things that make us human and the things that make us rooted. This piece was created for an exhibition that requested participants to make two chairs, one functional and the other conceptual. In my case I made them both non-functional, one soft and warm but lacking rear legs, the other hard and cold, lacking a place to sit. Placed together they function. As I played with them after they were built, I was surprised to discover that they also have this amazing relationship with one another. Depending on how they were composed, all sorts of aspects of their relationship were expressed.

It is in the nature of us human beings to look for clues to our own sense of place and belonging. Our environment and the way we live in the world is very important to this process. My final thought is this: being rooted is a necessary human condition. Your life partner, your family, your community, your country are all instinctive relationships that we nurture and need to be whole. We are each other's roots.

Peter Pierobon is a creative, innovative and internationally acclaimed artist with twenty-five years of experience inspired by the West Coast elements. His pieces are all meticulously handcrafted including combinations of metal, stone, and wood from local sources minimizing the environmental impact. Components for each piece are individually selected to create a finished product that is sculpturally resolved, structurally sound, and elegant—a masterpiece with a great story.

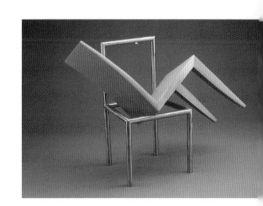

Judith Ames
Seattle, Washington

My interest in art and design began at a young age. The New England homes of my parents and grandparents contained examples of early American and European furniture. As a young person, I spent long hours engrossed in drawing and building imaginary worlds. In school and on my own time I sculpted and studied the works of Rodin, Matisse, the Fauvists, natural objects, and favorite architectural works. Although, while at Harvard and Colorado College (BA 1975), my academic classes were in philosophy, economics, and political science, furniture makers Sam Maloof and Art Carpenter and other excellent teachers inspired me to further studies in joinery, drafting, and design.

Instead of pursuing a degree in architecture right out of college, I chose a few years of practical experience. I found the work in a cabinet shop to be interesting in its own right and commenced a journey of learning the running of a business and the intricacies of wood construction. After a number of years my love of drawing led me from cabinetry to carvings and inlays in entry doors and cases. Those early images of animal and bird arcing around one another show the same fascination with the interplay of curved lines that has guided me in the subsequent years of furniture designs.

I grew up surrounded by treasured objects: be they a letter opener or a vase, they had story and meaning. They had been handed down by a relative, made by a special person, or purchased in a special place. In our work today, the challenges are ongoing. As we seek precision and efficiency in the processes of construction, grace and comfort in the look and function of a piece, we hope these new works will in turn be treasured.

Windswept Bench for Two, figured maple, western maple, 16" x 40" x 17.25". *Exhibited in association with FS14 at the Northwest Woodworkers Gallery, Seattle.*

Marc Brady Balentine
Fort Bragg, California

Heirloom Box, 2014, Cuban mahogany, big leaf maple, hard maple, 7" x 16" x 11". *2014 Faculty Selects Winner, Exhibited at FS14, the Port Townsend Chapel.*

Beston Barnett
San Diego, California

In 1996, I received my bachelor of science degree from Harvey Mudd College in engineering and sculpture. As an engineer, I worked at IBM for four years before leaving to pursue a career in the arts. While running Art Hurts Records—an independent music publisher—I attended the Cabinetry and Furniture Technology program at Palomar College, receiving awards from The Furniture Society, the San Diego Fine Woodworkers Association, and the North County Woodworking Club.

After getting my professional certificate in 2011, I joined the small community of craftspeople at Studio 6608 in San Diego and began furniture-making full time. Though the majority of my work is made on commission, I have shown speculative pieces at juried international shows in California and Washington.

The design of each new piece of furniture is a balancing act. Form and function are of course on the tightrope, but also strength and lightness, wood grain and geometry, elegance and surprise.

Maybe the trickiest balance in my own work is between modern rigor and ornament. I love the clean lines and paring down of the last half century, but I'm also fascinated by the world's older decorative traditions. Thus you'll find a walnut slab pierced by Maori-inspired motifs, or a floating cube sheathed in thirteenth-century Arabic carvings.

In the end, each piece is functional and must not only last a lifetime, but inspire a lifetime's use.

Mamluk Box, walnut, wenge, tamo ash, upholstery, 9" x 20" x 14". *Exhibited at FS14, the Port Townsend Chapel.*

Kufic Boxes, walnut, ebonized walnut, upholstery, 4" x 9" x 9". *Exhibited at FS14, the Port Townsend Chapel.*

Vivian Beer
Manchester, New Hampshire

Vivian Beer is a furniture designer/maker in New England. She tiptoes through contemporary design, craft, and sculptural aesthetics, sampling from each one. She deftly counterbalances a strong knowledge of contemporary furniture design with the history of industry and architecture to create furniture that intends to transform our expectations of and relationships to the domestic landscape with one-of-a-kind and limited production pieces. She is known for her fearless combinations of industrial materials in her furniture designs.

Beer's collections include the Smithsonian's Renwick Gallery, MFA Boston, and the Brooklyn Museum, public art for Portland ME and Cambridge MA. She holds an MFA from Cranbrook Academy of Art and was a resident artist at SUNY Purchase, SDSU, and Penland School in NC. As a research fellow at the Smithsonian Air and Space Museum, she studied the history of American aeronautical design as an inspiration for her next series of furniture.

Streamliner, 2014, formed and fabricated steel with automotive finish, 64" l x 16" w x 19.75" h. *Photo by Vivian Beer*

Anchored Candy No. 7, steel gun blue patina and automotive finish, 80" l x 22" w x 37" h. *Photo by Alison Swiatocha*

Anchored Candy No. 6, steel gun blue patina and automotive finish, 60" l x 21" w x 42" h. *Photo by Alison Swiatocha*

Nils Berg
Brooklyn, New York

Nils Berg is a designer and maker of fine furniture. He completed his formal training at the North Bennet Street School in Boston, where he graduated from the Cabinet and Furniture Making program in the spring of 2013. Nils lives and works in Brooklyn, New York.

Balston Chair, 2014, ash, leather, 31.75" h x 22" w x 22" d. *Photo by Adam Remion Williams*

Bruce Bradford
Winston Salem, North Carolina

Bruce Bradford is a furniture designer/craftsman who has enjoyed crafting unique works with an artistic and functional significance. His furniture uses decorative wood types and signature crafting methods to achieve an essence that is Bradford Custom Furniture.

Barstool, 2012, walnut & maple, 42" x 20.5" x 22". *Photos by Bruce P. Bradford*

Robert Brou
Atlanta, Georgia

I make furniture that I find exciting, full of motion and character. Works are carefully composed and complex creations that bring a beautiful piece of nature into your home. My focus is to continue creating designs that explore new forms from the natural world while always producing the finest functional yet sculptural organic furniture possible. Commissions for new or previous work are encouraged.

Wave Desk, walnut and MDF, 78" l x 34" w x 31" h.

Stoel Burrowes

Chapel Hill, North Carolina

I design and build fine furniture and art objects. Mostly, domestic hardwoods, but exotic woods, metals, glass, stone, paper, and a wide variety of hardware have been incorporated into my work. Modern and contemporary must include life, so I play in that zone of creative space between simplicity and ambiguity where archetype and generation reside. I bring fine craft together with history, human factors, poetry and play.

For the past ten years I also have been teaching. I am currently an assistant professor in the Department of Interior Architecture at the University of North Carolina at Greensboro. I infuse my teaching and mentoring with the research and scholarship of my practice.

"A"-Back Windsor, 2012, white oak, poplar, ash, milk paint, 34" x 28" x 22". *Photo by D. Smith*

Kristopher Chan
Seattle, Washington

Kristopher began building and designing furniture during a summer studio as an undergraduate at the University of Washington, from which he recently graduated in its master of architecture program. Kristopher designed and built *Alfred Bar Cabinet* while in a furniture studio at the UW co-taught by Kimo Griggs, faculty and designer, and Erling Christoffersen, a Danish furniture designer based in Copenhagen. A native of Seattle, Kristopher is influenced by industrial ruins and good typography, and is currently beginning his career in architecture.

Alfred Bar Cabinet, solid walnut and veneer, 35" x 35" x 18". *2014 Faculty Selects Winner, Exhibited at FS14, the Port Townsend Chapel.*

Shawn L. Connor
Harrisburg, Pennsylvania

Having studied furniture design and craftsmanship at Kutztown University in Pennsylvania and Buckinghamshire New University in England, Shawn Connor currently holds a BFA in crafts. He utilizes design and aesthetic to create inspired works. From the arched stance of a dog to the languid flow of a pepper leaf, Connor draws inspiration from familiar yet often overlooked objects to craft one-of-a-kind functional sculpture. Using experimental forms and textures, he engages the viewer on multiple levels of interest. Striving to maintain the feeling of or flow of movement that comes from the inspiring object, the form of the art piece is intended to intrigue the viewer before the practical function is realized. Connor is currently the principal of Connor Design-Build, LLC, in Harrisburg, Pennsylvania.

Puddle, 2014, Marmoleum top with inlaid wenge, cherry, and walnut; cherry skirt and legs, 48" l x 36" w x 18" h. *Photo by Dmitri Ganas*

Michael Cooper
Sebastopol, California

Michael Cooper was born in Richmond, California, and educated at San Jose State College, where he received a BA in commercial art and an MA in sculpture. He continued his studies at the University of California, Berkeley, where he earned an MFA. In addition to his creative work, he has taught at a number of colleges and universities, including UC-Berkeley, Foothill College in Los Altos, De Anza College in Cupertino, and the California College of Art in San Francisco. His work is in a number of private and public collections in the U.S. and internationally.

Hoppalong Cassidy Meets the Double Pussy with the Checkered Past, 2007, various hardwoods, steel, 46" x 36" x 30".

Modified, 2010, painted hard maple, anodized aluminum, chromed and painted steel, stainless steel, and mechanical components.

Matthew X. Curry
Bainbridge Island, Washington

Matthew X. Curry's MXC Design + Art is on Bainbridge Island near Seattle, Washington. His design work focuses on a "warm modernism"—a fusion of clean lines and Asian influences with an emphasis on natural materials, finely detailed and crafted.

Curry studied at the Pratt Institute School of Architecture in New York. His architectural training informs all areas of his multi-faceted career including interior and furniture design, as well as fine art drawings and sculpture.

The wood itself presents a wonderful and varied palette from bold to gentle, subtle to striking. Woodworking to me is a dialogue between the architectural and the organic. My approach to design in woodwork has completely reversed. In the past, I would draw designs to be executed by fine woodworkers. Now as a woodworker myself, wonderful woods and other materials become studies of how best they can be combined, milled and detailed to communicate a story.

Each sculptural piece becomes an exploration into material, design, and technique.

Moon + Mountain Entry Table, maple, walnut, wenge, other, 49.5" x 11" x 34". *Exhibited at FS14, the Port Townsend Chapel.*

John DeHoog
Ann Arbor, Michigan

John DeHoog's work references furniture and useful objects, without being bound to traditional forms. He treats wood as a somewhat mysterious material with eccentric qualities, balancing the physical and the visual. *Self-Leveling Cabinet* is a hybrid object that addresses both utility and futility.

DeHoog received his BFA (1996) from Northern Michigan University, and his MFA in furniture design (2000) from Rhode Island School of Design. His work has been shown nationally and internationally, and he currently exhibits throughout the greater Detroit area.

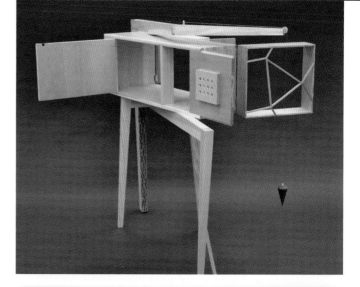

Self-Leveling Cabinet (closed & opened), 2012, fir, pine, palm, metal, 44" x 48" x 14". *Photo by John DeHoog*

David Delthony

Escalante, Utah

For over 30 years my life has been intertwined with the "Sculptured Furniture" I create. This endeavor has taken me from New York to West Berlin, Germany, where I earned my Master Cabinet Makers Certification and a degree in interior design at the Academy of Fine Arts. In 1996, I relocated to the canyon country of southern Utah, where my organic, sculptured forms find counterparts in the beauty of natural surroundings. My focus has been the dialog between functional and aesthetic values, balancing these in each object. As a studio furniture artist, my designs are sculpted in wood, utilizing inherent qualities of the material and my knowledge of ergonomics to create comfortable, functional organic forms. Within the concept and syntax of fine furniture, I infuse my work with an artistic sensuality, embracing visual and tactile senses and encourage the human contact defining my artistic vision.

All of my pieces are created by laminating wood, allowing stronger, complex designs. I currently use plywood, the material being extremely suitable for creating intricate cantilevered constructions. My intent is to combine artistic image (sculpture), function (ergonomics) and fine craftsmanship into organic, flowing forms and attempt to realize this through my own visual language.

Sculptured Chair III, 2013, laminated plywood, 32" x 36" x 27". *Photo by David Delthony*

Alicia Dietz
Richmond, Virginia

I recently traded a pilot helmet for a hand plane, following my passion for craft after a ten-year career as an officer and Blackhawk helicopter maintenance test pilot in the U.S. Army. I served in Iraq and have been stationed all over the world, including Germany, Alaska, and Egypt. While seemingly two different areas of expertise, my career in the army unexpectedly prepared me to design and build. The discipline necessary to command soldiers and to test broken helicopters has translated into an astute attention to detail and an unwavering work ethic.

I have accumulated many sources of inspiration from my years traveling and meeting a variety of people across the globe. As a woman, a soldier, and a dreamer, I have many experiences from which to draw, and I use those experiences to fuel my pieces. I employ a variety of media and techniques to include image transfers, encaustics, and glass to enhance my furniture pieces. Always looking for a new experiment, I find the journey of the creative process its own reward.

I earned a BSJ in advertising/journalism from Ohio University in 2001 and two woodworking and furniture making degrees from Vermont Woodworking School in 2012 and 2013.

Come Fly Away with Me, 2013, red birch, basswood, maple, walnut, milk paint, image transfer, glass, encaustics, wire, string, handmade paper, ink, 102" x 28" x 4". *Photo by Amanda Lass*

Through the Looking Glass, 2013, ash, tempered glass, black dye, liming wax, oil, polyurethane, 59" x 26" x 18". *Photo by Amanda Lass*

Tom & Jennifer Dolese
Bellingham, Washington

Tom Dolese was born on the Navaho Reservation in Ganado, Arizona. He was five when his family moved to Anchorage, Alaska, where he grew up. After college, while doing geophysics research in Yellowstone Park, Tom built a small scribe-fit log cabin on land owned by his family in the Beartooth Mountains and realized he was more interested in creating furniture than working as a geophysicist. After meeting Jennifer, he moved to Missoula, Montana, where he set up a woodworking shop and started designing and building furniture. Currently, Tom builds gallery and commission pieces and teaches woodworking in his Bellingham, Washington, studio.

Jennifer Dolese grew up in Missoula, Montana. She attended Willamette University for two years, then the University of Regensburg in Germany for a year before finishing up at the University of Montana with degrees in English and environmental studies. Jennifer worked for the YMCA, the Montana Natural History Center, Clark Fork School, and then enjoyed being a full-time mom when her daughter, Sarah, was born. As her husband, Tom, started designing and building furniture, Jennifer took classes in stained and leaded glass design. She began building commissioned pieces, often collaborating with Tom. Jennifer expanded into the art of marquetry (pictures made with wood veneers) after taking a course at the Anderson Ranch Art Center from marquetarian Craig Vandall Stevens. Jennifer has been working as an artisan for eighteen years. Her work is influenced by the Arts and Crafts movement, the Prairie style, geometric images, other artists, and the organic lines and patterns of nature.

Tom and Jennifer Dolese are members of the Artwood Gallery in Bellingham, Washington, and The Northwest Woodworkers Gallery in Seattle, Washington.

Adjustable Backed Chair with Ottoman, fabric, curly maple, 28" x 28" x 38". *Exhibited at FS14, the Port Townsend Chapel.*

Pinecone Marquetry Cabinet, maple, curly maple, sapele, walnut, burl walnut, 12" x 7" x 22.5". *Exhibited at FS14, the Port Townsend Chapel.*

Salish Sea Marquetry Lantern, cherry, glass, 10" x 10" x 17". *Exhibited in association with FS14 at the Northwest Woodworkers Gallery, Seattle.*

William Doub
Deerfield, New Hampshire

I have lived and worked in northern New England off and on since 1974. It allows me the solitude and open space to focus on my work, and the opportunity to draw upon asymmetric and symmetric forms, textures, and tonalities found fresh and unfiltered in this natural place.

Since graduating from the Furniture Programs at North Bennett Street School in Boston, and the University of New Hampshire Wood Design in the early 1970s, I have been exclusively self-employed in my chosen profession as a designer and builder of fine custom furniture for over forty years. Early in my career I established a specialization in Art Nouveau-style furniture, with added influences from Japanese art, and Arts and Crafts design.

I have, however, evolved my own motifs and structures from nature and my subconscious. The parquetry appliques and marquetry panels are drawn directly from nature, and then built into pieces of furniture. As I walk in the woods, I collect branches, knots, antlers, and rocks that inspire my designs. I use burls when I can, and seek out unusual veneers that emphasize the organic growth lines and character of the wood.

I continue to learn a great deal from every challenge, working to keep my mind open to new forms evolving out of high technology. I follow the work of organic and post-modern architects from Frank Gehry to Zaha Hadid, who use technology extensively to simulate and generate their visions of next and better worlds to come.

Art Nouveau Breakfront, 2010, curly maple and walnut, 90" w x 22" d x 84" h. *Photo by William Doub*

Mystic Bed, 2012, curly maple and walnut, 74" w x 85" d x 72" h. *Photo by William Doub*

Tor and Robert Erickson
Nevada City, California

Just months after graduating from college in 1969, Robert Erickson hitchhiked to California to follow his dream of becoming a furniture maker. On arriving in California, he met renowned poet Gary Snyder, who invited the Nebraskan to spend a summer helping him build a house in the foothills of the Sierra Nevada.

Inflamed with idealism at the end of the project, Erickson and other young, talented members of Snyder's construction crew banded together to buy a large neighboring parcel. In 1973, he built the first structure on the land—a woodshop that he has worked in ever since. Over the next four decades, Erickson and his land partners have built their houses, families, and lives on the piece of land they still share.

In 1978, Robert married Liese Greensfelder and a year later they had their only child. Tor grew up in and around the woodshop, learning how to work the tools, mill a log with a two-man chainsaw mill, and understand the different properties of bigleaf maple, Pacific madrone, and other local woods. Tor left for college, lived in the Pacific Northwest and worked in Africa, but always came back to help his father in the shop. In 2014, he became a full partner in the business with his parents.

Robert and Tor aspire to design and create furniture that is enduring, functional, and beautiful to behold. They are perhaps best known for their individually tailored chairs—many featuring the "floating back" invented by Robert in 1975—and for Tor's innovative new table designs.

Today Robert and Tor work with two other craftsmen in the original shop to make some seventy-five pieces of furniture a year, building each by hand, one at a time. Their work is represented in various collections, including the Smithsonian American Art Museum's Renwick Gallery, the Los Angeles County Museum of Art, Racine Art Museum and the Yale University Art Gallery.

Tashjian Chair, Pacific yew, turned manzanita finials, brass hinges and bushings, free-range bison leather, 25" x 28" x 42". *Exhibited in association with FS14 at the Northwest Woodworkers Gallery, Seattle.*

Michael Fitzpatrick
Westborough, Massachusetts

Born in 1962, Michael Fitzpatrick has been working with his hands from a young age. Witnessing his grandfather, a farmer, furniture maker, and housewright, Fitzpatrick was influenced in a personal, profound, and lifelong way. Growing up in Suffern, New York, on his grandfather's farm, living in a post-and-beam barn that was restored, appointed, and furnished by his grandfather gave Fitzpatrick a rare insight to hands-on potential.

After attending the University of New Hampshire and Boston University College of Engineering, Fitzpatrick began to rebuild buildings in Boston in his grandfather's manner, doing all the work himself with a hand-selected crew. He learned many trades in the house building industry becoming most proficient in woodworking. In 1989, he moved to Marblehead, Massachusetts, a quaint, seaside community, where he set up a small shop nestled in "Old Burial Hill." Here, he began making custom cabinets, wood furniture, and finish work for the old historic houses of Marblehead.

In 2004, Fitzpatrick attended the full time, two-year furniture program at the North Bennet Street School in Boston to refine and further his furniture making skills. After graduation he set up a studio in Boston and makes his furniture pieces one at at time for his clients.

Michael Fitzpatrick moved his shop from Boston to Westborough, MA in 2012. The barn/studio is part of his award-winning restoration project where he resides with his wife, Dr. Jean Keamy.

La Violinista, 2011, wenge, figured ash, painted ash, 48" h, 15" w, 10" d. *Photo by Jean Keamy*

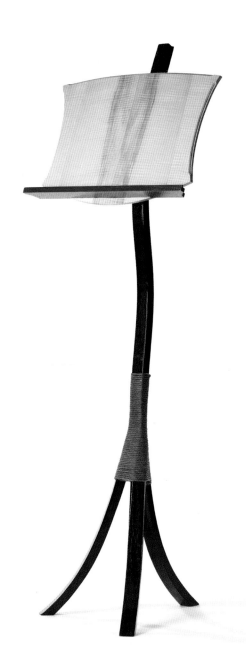

MICHAEL FITZPATRICK FURNITURE MAKER, LLC
43 Church Street Westborough, MA 01581
(781) 258-7485
www.BostonFurnitureMaker.com
www.43ChurchSt.com
MFitz@BostonFurnitureMaker.com

David Fleming
Scottsdale, Arizona

I make wood furniture and objects that combine function, craft, and design. Having been a student of James Krenov in the early 1980s, I am drawn to the same subtle lines, proportions, and expressive use of the natural qualities of wood that he advocated, as well as the emphasis on craft and hand work that was his hallmark.

Spalted Wall Cabinet, 2013, Honduras mahogany, spalted maple, Port Orford cedar, pau ferro, 22" h x 12" w x 5" d. *Photos by David Fleming*

Small Cherry Box, cherry, Port Orford cedar, desert ironwood, 4" x 6" x 10". *Exhibited at FS14, the Port Townsend Chapel.*

green wood chairs

ALISON OSPINA

I received an invitation last January to attend the Annual Furniture Society Conference taking place at the Port Townsend School of Woodworking, Washington State.

Lee Valley Tools and Freshwood Publishing kindly sponsored my travel to the U.S. It was a long journey from southwest Ireland, via Heathrow, Vancouver, and finally, a car ferry to Port Townsend, one of the myriad West Coast islands in the Puget Sound.

The Furniture Society's annual conference takes place in different parts of the country each year. In 2014, it was the turn of Washington State, and the Port Townsend School of Woodworking offered to host the event. The School is based in Fort Worden State Park, which was a military fort from the late 1800s until World War II. Functioning now as a conference center, conference attendees were housed very comfortably in Victorian Officers' Quarters—large, balloon-framed houses with covered porches running along the sides and front, all built around what used to be the central parade ground.

This year's theme "Rooted—Creating a Sense of Place" was intended to explore the connection between furniture makers and their communities. Using the example of the artisan food movement, makers were challenged to find ways of connecting with local markets and making use of the timber produced in their local region. They were also asked to consider what links their work with the locality; for example, do vernacular furniture styles exist historically? Are the natural contours and colours in the landscape reflected in the creative work produced there?

I live and work in West Cork, Ireland, a place that is defined by its coastal landscapes and the Atlantic Ocean. Since the 1960s, a community of artists and craftspeople has grown up here, alongside a vibrant artesan food movement, earning the region a reputation for its high quality, innovative products and creations.

Green Wood Chairs literally begin life "rooted" in the landscape in the form of hazel trees that grow, self-sown, along many field boundaries and roads. The trees are coppiced during the winter months, ready to be made into chairs during the spring and summer. Since 1998, I have been teaching between twenty and thirty students per year to make their own green wood chairs, which can be seen for sale in local craft shops and farmers' markets from Bantry to Kinsale.

Green Wood Chairs (the business) is so rooted in West Cork that if I lived elsewhere, I am sure that I would be making something different. Here I find the inspiration, the material, the opportunity, the market, and the potential to spread the word in an atmosphere of creative experiment and excitement.

Even though I was attending with a "Green Wood Chairs" agenda and, at first, positively avoiding sessions about digital fabrication, I found myself increasingly intrigued by the possibilities the world of 3-D printers and CNC routers offers. Firstly, I must admit to having to ask what a CNC router is—it is the kind of technology to which I would normally pay no attention, as it seems to have no connection with green wood construction. There may be woodworkers out there who know as little about CNC routers as I did.

In a nutshell, it is a computer-controlled cutting machine, similar to a hand-held router, but able to produce precise, high quality work at high speed. It is automated and can accurately cut mortise and tenon joints as well as perform tasks that would normally be done by panel saws, pillar drills, and spindle molders. It is as efficient in making a one-off piece as it is for a run of identical items. Designs are uploaded to the computer via a CAD program.

During the coffee break I found myself chatting with Gustavo Bonet, a recent graduate of the Graduate School of Architecture, Planning, and Preservation, at Columbia University. In January 2014, he set up a company using CNC routers to fabricate architectural features, furniture, and what he describes as "homeware." Although I was not totally sold on some of his design ideas, I kept coming back to the thought that a CNC router could easily be programmed to create the perfectly scooped-out wooden chair seat again and again, a job that takes me hours and that I am rarely satisfied with.

The next presentation I attended was entitled "The Zen Chair." I can never resist anything with "chairs" in the title and soon found myself in a packed class room listening to Tak Yoshino from Yamanashi, Japan. Tak explained that his wife had been ill for many years and as a result he had been inspired to create a piece of furniture that would positively impact people's health.

According to Tak, too many of us lead sedentary lives and spend long hours sitting in badly designed chairs. If the pelvis, shoulders, and spine are not correctly aligned, an unequal pressure is created along the spine and back. Over time this can cause tension headaches, disc problems, and pain in the lower back and shoulders. When making a chair for a particular person, Tak measures their body and makes adjustments around major (acupuncture) pressure points until he finds the best position for the pelvis, allowing the spine to maintain its natural curve.

Tak has designed the Zen Chair based on his practical understanding of both Zen and chiropractic theory. The chairs are made of beautifully figured Japanese timber and are sculpted to ensure the best fit for the human body. Tak uses over 300 tiny handmade planes called "kanna" to create delicate curves, allowing him to fit the chair around the physique of individual clients.

Tak brought three examples of his "Zen Chairs" to exhibit at the conference and we were allowed to try them out. They really lived up to the hype. They are beautifully made and very comfortable, obliging you to sit in the correct, "healthy" position. Considering that I was suffering with severe lower back pain throughout the entire three days, I wanted one of those chairs—I really did!

As I had been invited to present my own Green Wood Chairs business and run two workshops, I was surprised to find that I was one of only a handful of green woodworkers attending the conference. The Pacific Northwest has enormous tracts of privately owned forest as well as state and national parks; there is no shortage of trees, but there definitely is a shortage of people working with unseasoned branch wood.

Having attended presentations by several well-respected furniture makers, I was beginning to wonder how my own work would be viewed. It is just so different. These guys are producing contemporary furniture made from exotic timbers, in high tech workshops, using every modern machine and device known to man, and the work was technically outstanding.

My whole approach is very different. I use what I describe as "appropriate technology," i.e. two or three hand-held power tools and an array of hand tools. I only make mortice and tenon joints, and I allow the materials to dictate. I make the chairs I have the sticks for—not the other way round. My designs are simple, my intention is to intervene as little as possible between the tree and the completed chair or stool. The tree has done the hard work, growing beautiful, sinuous branches—it is my job to select, peel and join them, creating a functional seat that best displays the beauty of the wood.

In any event, my two workshops were well attended, and I was delighted to discover that woodworkers of any ilk seem to enjoy the challenge of making a green wood stool in just two hours, especially if they can take it home! Most people attending the workshops had some background in fabricating—whether it be with wood, plastic, or man-made board. They understood how to make 3-D objects.

Tim Lawson, director of the Port Townsend School, very kindly delegated Abel Isaac Dances to assist me in organizing the workshops. He had a copy of my book, and we liaised via email during the spring, while he was coppicing alder for the workshops. The alder was growing on his own woodland, and he sent me the occasional photo just to check that he had the right dimensions and quantities. He acquired some very attractive 10" cherry board for the stool tops.

Abel did a fantastic job, and I arrived to find the workshop set up with benches, tools, and equipment ready to use—plus all tools were clean and incredibly sharp! Lee Valley Tools had generously offered to supply a range of tenoners in various sizes, we had all the space and equipment we needed.

I took along my own 15mm and 18mm DISSTON Multi-Angle drill bits (purchased from Screwfix) and I am greatly relieved that I did, because the school had not managed to source MAD (or "3-D") bits in advance. These bits drill cleanly into green wood with no problems, where other drill bits struggle, snag, and ultimately fail.

A group of around twelve people turned up for the first workshop. I always hope that my enthusiasm will be infectious, but I know it is necessary to first describe and explain how it all works. However, this group seemed to grasp the principles straight away. Once I had shown them "one I made earlier" (which I took flat-packed in my suitcase) and given brief instructions, they just dived in.

When describing the green wood method, which for me is a passion, I can never be certain that people will understand, straight away, why it is so exciting. They often begin tentatively, trying it out, following my directions, hoping not to do anything "wrong" but there always comes a point when the excitement kicks in and they start to smile. They begin to see the possibilities and feel liberated by not having to follow the usual rules or look for square, or measure in millimeters. It is a special moment when the "green wood approach" just clicks.

Before I knew it, the two hours had flown by and we had a multitude of finished and half-finished stools in a variety of dimensions, on the bench. The following day some people came back to put the finishing touches to their work, while word had spread about the workshop and another group turned up to embark on another two-hour green wood stool project.

Some of the workshop attendees were people who make bespoke furniture to a very high standard for a living. Watching them discover the fun of working with unseasoned alder, as if it were a new material, different to what they normally use, made me wonder: If creating something from wood is a source of pleasure— could producing something from green wood be a higher pleasure?

Alison Ospina has been chair-making in West Cork since 1996, using locally coppiced hazel wood. She is a member of a local guild of craftspeople in West Cork and teaches her craft from her own studio and also at a local college. She is author of the book Green Wood Chairs *(2009).*

Reuben Foat
San Diego, California

Reuben is from Mukwonago, Wisconsin, a small town outside Milwaukee. He discovered furniture-making in the spring of 2003 while attending the University of Wisconsin–Madison and has been working in the field ever since.

Foat's experience spans from cabinet making in the United Kingdom and New England, to restoring furniture in Milwaukee, Wisconsin. He recently finished an MFA degree at San Diego State University with an emphasis in furniture design and digital fabrication. Now, in addition to being a furniture designer and maker, he is a teacher.

Foat is a passionate object maker and continually seeks out opportunities to teach others. He has taught at art/craft centers across the country including the Center for Furniture Craftsmanship, Anderson Ranch Arts Center, and Haystack Mountain School of Crafts. He has been a lecturer at the University of Massachusetts Dartmouth, San Diego State University, and Cuyamaca College in California, where he now lives. He currently is the makers teacher at High Tech Middle Media Arts.

Being well-acquainted with traditional furniture making techniques and being a digital fabrication enthusiast, Foat strives to elegantly combine these divergent methods in his studio practice and in his classroom. Technologies that include computer-aided-design (CAD) and computer-aided-manufacturing (CAM) are standard at the industrial level of object making. These technologies offer compelling opportunities to makers of all levels and mediums.

Rodeo Chair, walnut, plywood, 18" x 18" x 28". *Exhibited at FS14, the Port Townsend Chapel.*

Bryan Geary
Dartmouth, Massachusetts

I have chosen the discipline of sculptural furniture because it allows me to speak through familiar and intuitive objects. I believe these common symbols are something that most people can relate to. They are reminiscent of family dinners, date nights with a loved one, spiritual gatherings, and political summits. I like to take simple ideas and put a twist on them. Tables are both symbolic and functional. They support and unite us through life's twists and turns, as we build together or watch as things fall apart.

Rift is made from book-matching a natural-edged tiger maple slab. The distress at the middle of the table creates a physical obstruction between two chairs, alluding to a couple in a distressed relationship. The chairs rising through the table's surface and the damage prevent the use of the table in a traditional manner. The spalt and cracking in the tiger maple indicate that the piece has been worn down over time. This once-pristine piece has developed stresses and has begun to erode, mimicking the effects of time and stress on intimacy.

A furniture designer and maker, Bryan Geary was born in northwest Pennsylvania. He completed his BFA and MFA in furniture design at the University of Massachusetts Dartmouth and now resides in Kawaguchiko as a deshi (apprentice) under furniture maker, Master Takahiro Yoshino.

Rift, spalted tiger maple & ash, 55" h x 36" w x 17.5". *2014 Faculty Selects Winner.*

Andrew Glantz
Scottsdale, Arizona

Andrew Glantz is a furniture designer and maker who lives and works in Scottsdale, Arizona. Born and raised on the East Coast, he attended Wesleyan University for both his BA and masters degrees. After teaching graphic arts for ten years, Glantz turned to period piece renovation and construction in 1978, and then, in 1984, when he moved West, he began to devote his efforts solely to contemporary, sculptural furniture design and construction. He is owner of Zenith Design, a one person studio, and is responsible for all phases of design, construction, and marketing. Glantz was tapped to serve as a trustee of The Furniture Society starting in 2005, and served as treasurer, vice president and president, as well as chair of the Development Committee. His term ended in 2011, but he remains an active and involved member.

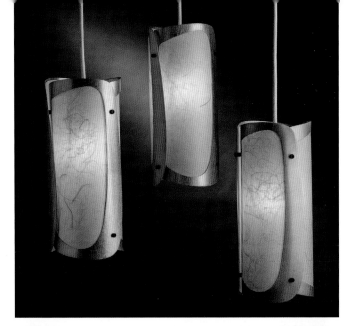

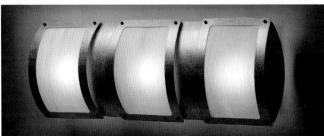

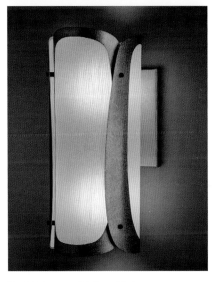

Zenith Copper Lights, 2013, copper, laminated shoji paper, electrical parts, steel machine screws. Pendant light: 4.5" diam. x 11" h; vanity light: 20" w x 4" deep x 7.5" h; wall sconce: 4.5" w x 5.5" deep x 11" h. *Photos by Dan Delaney, 2D Photography*

Casa de Colibri Dining Tables, 2013, bubinga, wenge. Main table: 52" w at center x 96" l x 28" h; side tables: 24" w x 42"–51" l x 28" h. *Photos by Dan Delaney, 2D Photography*

Glen Guarino
Cedar Grove, New Jersey

I hope my furniture speaks clearly, in a language that conveys a sense of the person behind the art; of someone who loves the creative process and respects the beauty of the material from which it is made. As each viewer moves a hand along the lines of the work, I want them to sense the skill and love for the craft needed to create it.

For me, each new design is a small adventure, exploring my imagination and the potential of the material. Like craftsmen of the past, I prefer to perform my work using fine hand tools instead of relying on machines that may technically speed completion, but limit the scope of the design. Machines, while certainly useful at times, can create an artificial distance between the artist and the material. My hands-on approach allows me to let the simplicity of the design reveal itself, creating a piece that imparts serenity and calm, reflecting the tree's grace and strength. As each design becomes real and tangible, I get a sense of a tree evolving into a new life as a useful piece of art. I'm grateful to be the catalyst for this rebirth.

Storm, 2009, northern catalpa (top), ash (base), both rescued, 28" h x 37.5" w x 29.75" d. *Photo by Justin Guarino Photography*

Bianca, 2004, rescued northern catalpa, 28" h x 19" w x 36.75" *Photo by Justin Guarino Photography*

Michael Hamilton
Port Hadlock, Washington

Wood is a bridge between nature and material culture. Nature, as observed in the macro to micro continuum, is a primary source of inspiration; color, texture, order, form as well as raw material. As a child the why of appearance was of consuming interest for me. It prompted my exploration of history and culture, through objects crafted of wood— objects as diverse as basic kitchenware, sophisticated royal seating, or evocative North Coast totems. Motif, detail, and pattern as cultural symbol bring meaning, give objects context. As I began to work with wood the why was joined by the quest for technique; and eventually, the understanding of appropriate application of technique and how technique, in itself, contributes to appearance.

Over time, my personal aesthetic has developed as an applied response to symbolism, technique, design refinement, a healthy interest in experimentation, and a desire to work with the inherent qualities of wood as a medium. This response has guided me on an endless journey involving many knowledgeable and inspiring teachers, mentors, and colleagues. I am especially thankful that my experience as a maker has provided such a rich and diverse connection to our life and times. I look forward to many more years of cultural exploration with wood as the vehicle.

"Perch" Stool, Oregon walnut, 26" x 17" x 17". *Exhibited at FS14, the Port Townsend Chapel.*

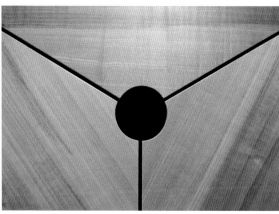

"Feast Bowl" Occasional Table, Oregon walnut & Pacific big leaf maple, 43" x 43" x 18". *Exhibited in association with FS14 at the Northwest Woodworkers Gallery, Seattle.*

Rob Hare
Ulster Park, New York

Forty years ago, I started out with an MFA to be a sculptor and pursued this dream for twenty years, while also doing carpentry, welding, construction, and cabinetry to make ends meet. Clients would see my sculpture in wood and metal and say: "If you can make that you could make me furniture." They were right. I could and did, and slowly came to realize that the furniture I was designing answered many of my sculptural needs and more. In particular, my furniture is expected to be touched and that added both an emotional connection and a patina that cannot be attained in any other way. My furniture is made and designed to be used and enjoyed with the structural elements creating a full round sculptural form. For the past two decades I have only made furniture. Many clients are now close friends and when I visit them I am sometimes hard pressed to find something in their home I have not made.

Watch Hill Sideboard, 2010, tiger figured ash, hand-forged steel, three drawers on full extension drawer slides, 75" l x 18" d x 36" h. *Photos by Chris Kendall*

Twist Elliptical Dining Table, 2012, four-plank top, book-matched & grain-matched eastern walnut, hand-forged solid aluminum base, anodized, 72" l x 42" w x 28" h. *Photos by Chris Kendall*

Alan Harp
Lilburn, Georgia

Alan Harp works under the premise of "what you want doesn't exist... yet." Educated in industrial design with over twenty years of experience creating custom products and furniture, he strives to create pieces to fulfill his client's specific wishes. The goal of Alan Harp Design is to provide clients with that unique piece that can't be purchased elsewhere, while also digging into the past to re-create and restore family heirlooms.

Prior to the creation of Alan Harp Design, Harp served as the furniture instructor for the College of Architecture at Georgia Tech where his students were frequently featured in national competitions. Utilizing his experience in teaching, Harp now has an apprentice in the shop to help bring a new generation into the furniture design field. Alan Harp Design is in Lilburn, Georgia.

White Oak and Padauk Ping Pong Table, 2014, white oak and padauk veneers over a Baltic birch substrate, 60" w x 108" l x 30" h. *Photo by Alan Harp*

Peter Harrison
Middle Grove, New York

The style of my furniture grew out of a desire to build without traditional woodworking joinery. This began as a method of making furniture, but quickly became integral to the composition and design of my work. I use three materials: wood, mtal, and concrete. Each has characteristics that are specifically suited for different elements. The aesthetic nature of the elements long ago became more important than their convenience.

My designs break from traditional furniture forms. It is rare that I build a table with four legs. Decorative components made from stainless steel cables or rods are used as important visual elements. I find these elements give life to my pieces. Pure minimalism errs toward being boring. My work celebrates materials and maintains a pure feeling that is modern without being devoid of details.

Redux Chair, 2012, maple, red lacquer, aluminum, 31" x 15" x 18". *Photos by Stockstudiosphotography.com*

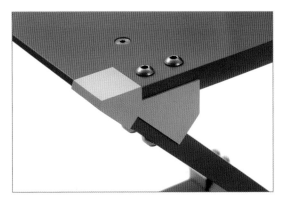

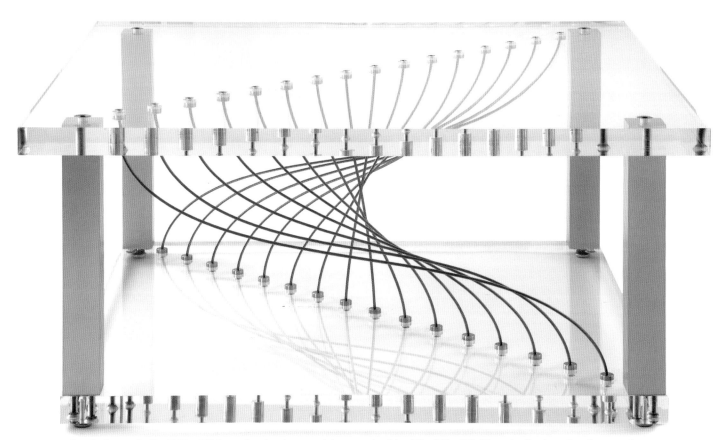

Acrylic Argon Coffee Table, 2014, acrylic, aluminum, stainless steel cable, 16" x 36" x 36". *Photo by Stockstudiosphotography.com*

Sabina Hill

Port Moody, British Columbia

Sabina Hill, in collaboration with aboriginal artists, creates original custom furniture, art, and installations that merge the rich mythology of West Coast native culture with a contemporary design aesthetic. Hill skillfully integrates Native motifs into her work creating a unique, contemporary expression, one that evokes the natural beauty of the Pacific Northwest and celebrates the convergence of two distinct design cultures.

The native motifs are created in collaboration with local artists: Andy Everson, Mark Preston, and Steve Smith, Corinne Hunt, and recently, Jessica Silvey. Her work is handcrafted locally, utilizing unique material combinations and leading edge technologies. These handcrafted, museum quality works are authenticated limited editions and commissions that showcase an ever-expanding palette of materials, which reflect her highly collectible and evolving design aesthetic.

Salmon Drum Tables, salmon skin, walnut, and red cedar, 15" diam. x 22" h; coho, 15" diam. x 18" h; cedar, 18" diam. x 15" h.

Feast Sideboard—Whale, with Mark Preston. The whale motif is cut through the oak revealing an eighth-inch depth highlighted by an ebonized oak backing, 72" l x 18" w x 26.75" h. Limited Edition 10.

Bear Wall Panel—Spirit Bear, with Andy Everson. Custom high gloss white lacquer and matte finish with solid white oak frame, 61.5" w x 61.5" h x 2.25" d. Limited Edition 10.

Thunderbird Chairs, with Andy Everson, solid walnut and hand-sewn Italian leather with diamond tufted detailing, 34.75" d x 36.5" w x 31" w. Limited Edition 10.

Jake Hockel
Austin, Texas

My work is heavily influenced by the writings of James Krenov, as well as the experience I gained during two years of study at the College of the Redwoods Fine Woodworking Program in Fort Bragg, California.

I am a strong proponent of creative responsibility and feel that, in an age when the world is sinking under the weight of so much stuff, people with an inclination to add to the amount of it should strive to make good stuff.

I think of good stuff as being work crafted for planned endurance instead of obsolescence, emanating from a personal vision and looking better in real life than it does on the internet. It has a purpose and serves it beautifully for a long time.

I have a small shop outside Austin, Texas, where I strive to make good stuff for people who appreciate it.

Untitled (Desk), eastern walnut, European beech, California acacia, 29" x 44" x 18". *2014 Faculty Selects Winner, Exhibited at FS14, the Port Townsend Chapel.*

54

Stephen Hogbin
Georgian Bluffs, Ontario, Canada

Stephen Hogbin's primary residence is in a woodland near Lake Charles, Ontario. He graduated from the Royal College of Art in London, England. In 1970, he began to work as a studio artist while instructing at Sheridan College and University of Toronto. Hogbin has been a member of The Royal Canadian Academy since 1983. In 2013, he received the Queen Elizabeth II, Diamond Jubilee Medal.

Hogbin exhibits widely in North America and beyond. He exhibited at the Art Gallery of Ontario 1975 in an exhibition titled *Chairs*. Subsequently these pieces were purchased by Yale University Art Gallery and the Minneapolis Institute for the Arts. He has exhibited at the Museum of Civilization, Ottawa; National Museum of American Art, Renwick Gallery, Washington; and Australian National University, Canberra. There have been thirty-six solo exhibitions and over two hundred group exhibitions in Australia, Canada, Europe, Japan, Korea and the U.S.

Wine Table for a Cottage, 2014, ash, maple, birch, paint, 30" x 58" x 14". *Photo by Stephen Hogbin*

Hank Holzer
Seattle, Washington

Hank Holzer, a designer, builder and mentor for younger woodworkers, found his passion for working with wood at a young age and continues to enjoy the endless possibilities that designing in wood offers. He became a member of Northwest Fine Woodworking Gallery shortly after its founding and has served there as board member, president and juror for many years. He manages the well maintained and finely tuned wood shop where he, wife Judith, and seven others woodworkers wield their woodworking craft. He does some teaching of newer members, but his main passion remains building.

Wabi-Sabi Bench, madrone, 48" x 13" x 24". *Exhibited in association with FS14 at the Northwest Woodworkers Gallery, Seattle.*

Rocking Akira Chair, claro walnut, 22" x 17" x 36". *Exhibited at FS14, the Port Townsend Chapel..*

Katie Hudnall
Indianapolis, Indiana

My pieces are metaphors for our relationships with one another. The imperfect edge of one piece fitting perfectly against the imperfect edge of another, pieces whose function suggest protection but offer no real security, and everything seemingly on the verge of collapse, but never quite collapsing. I am tapping into the delight that comes from seeing something work that shouldn't, the hope that comes from a thing endlessly repaired, no matter how many times it has broken, and the beauty in something textured with imperfections and then worn smooth through use.

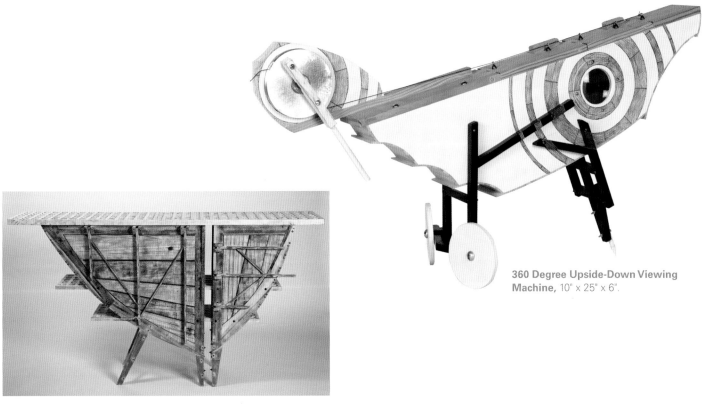

360 Degree Upside-Down Viewing Machine, 10" x 25" x 6".

Spirits Cabinet, 2011, found/salvaged wood, hardware, paint, wax, 60" l x 36" t x 16" d. *Photos by Michelle Given*

57

Matt Hutton
Portland, Maine

My work explores process, utility, and form. It also focuses on the transformation of the Midwest landscape, particularly that of farmlands that have deteriorated due to inactivity and redevelopment. These works are also inspired by the idea of nostalgia, independency/dependency, fossils, barns and grain silos, water towers, roadway billboards, and other architectural elements that have interest in mass, volume, and gravity and riddle this landscape. While often dilapidated and degenerate, these architectural landmarks continue to endure amongst the contemporary sprawl and it is from these that I pull information of time, history, layers, and information of structure and construction to create functional objects.

Table & Mirror, 2014, bubinga, wenge & maple, 82" x 72" x 24". *Photo by Adam Manley*

Spiritual Center, Prayer Wall, located at Maine General Hospital in Augusta, 2013, catalpa, ash & walnut, 18' x 18' x 2'. *Photo by Adam Manley*

Crop Circles, 2014, maple, 53" x 53" x 16". *Photo by Jonathan Theodorou*

Craig Johnson
St. Paul, Minnesota

Perfection in craft is never achievable, yet always worthy of pursuit.

Woodworking and furniture-making challenge me to balance overall composition with close attention to the most minute details. Every shape and line has intention. Every surface and edge has been touched and cared for. I strive to let the grain of the wood speak for itself, while juxtaposing the more rigid geometries of the man-made world beside the natural aspects of the wood. So, in a very personal way, each piece is a quiet celebration and reminder of the intimate relationship that exists between us and nature.

Properly tuned hand tools, a deep appreciation for the chosen material, and a calm, sensitive approach to design and to the making itself all combine to set the tone for my work.

Jeffersonian Book Stand, 2011, yellow birch, bird's eye maple and shop-made brass brackets, 16" h x 13.5" w x 13.5" d (closed); 25.52" h x 32.625" w x 32.625" d (fully opened). *Photo by Studio Tupla*

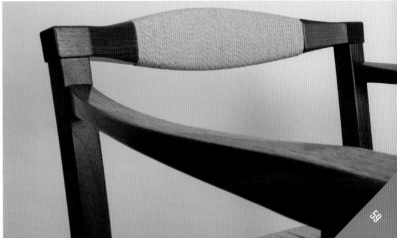

Black Walnut Armchair, 2013, locally grown black walnut and Danish cord, 28.125" h x 22" w x 18.25" d. *Photo by Studio Tupla*

Gary Jonland
Port Townsend, Washington

After twenty-five years as a cabinetmaker and custom furniture maker in Port Townsend, I strive to design pieces that will connect the right form with the right wood and create works of enduring beauty and usefulness. I love simple, clean lines and believe that furniture and cabinetry design (proportion and composition) should serve the natural beauty of wood, allowing the qualities of the chosen material (color, subtle textures, inherent boldness) to take the foreground. I tend toward a modernist aesthetic, much like that of the Scandinavian modernists who are masters of exceptional, spare designs that provide both a minimalist framework and an elegant effect. At the same time, I remain interested in all facets of classical architecture and their influence on the history of furniture.

I am a native of Chicago, a former Olympic speed skater, and an avid golfer and skier. Since moving to Washington's Olympic Peninsula over two decades ago, I have rooted myself in Port Townsend's unique community of artists, craftsmen, and wooden boatbuilders. I've created custom cabinetry and furniture for individual clients and organizations throughout the Pacific Northwest.

Luna, painted maple and bird's eye maple, 33" x 62" x 18". *Exhibited at FS14, the Port Townsend Chapel.*

Danny Kamerath
Kerrville, Texas

I approach designing and making furniture in simple terms. I try to make things that are elegant and beautiful to look at, pleasing to touch, and sturdy to use. I use wood that is appropriate for the piece. With the right strength and structural properties, the right color, and pleasing grain, I try to design with the knowledge that glue will someday fail so the joiner must be able to support the piece and the people who use it. And I work hard to make the scale and proportions of the piece feel right.

Debbi, 2013, wenge, sepele, padauk, rosewood, bubinga, beeswing figured satin wood, tiger maple, African mahogany, Baltic birch plywood, annigre, birds' eye maple, striped ebony, Gabon ebony, purpleheart, cherry, and brass, 53" x 34" x 18". *Photo by Danny Kamerath*

Peter Kasper

Tiffin, Iowa

My work tells stories about the relationships between people and materials. "Materials" and "story" are symbiotically related in my work. One cannot exist without the other. I gather these stories through close observation and share them through my craft. I strive to tell each material's history and yet leave an opening for viewers to integrate their own thoughts with a piece.

When I work, I connect with the wood. Close inspection of the raw material communicates a story. Details such as grain patterns, checks, nail holes, mineral streaks, spalting, knots, and burls reveal a timeline in the life of the materials. These are the components of the wood's story to be told. Inspiration for a piece may come from the defining characteristics and an urge to share these characteristics.

In other cases, materials are chosen for their general traits. Then the wood tells a more literal or sculptural story. In this instance, materials are selected to carry the plot. Each genre of materials comes with a set of cultural meanings pertaining to its region, uses and value. Understanding the cultural meanings enables the viewer to shape a story through interactions with their own ideas.

When I create, I wish to link the material and viewer through a story and a shared experience.

Family Tree Table, 2011, white oak, walnut, oil, milk paint, found objects, 30" h x 18" diam. *Photo by George Ensley*

Mad-zen Case Study, 2013, white oak, walnut, oil, 42" h x 18" w x 12" d. *Photo by Tanya Clowers*

61

Clark Kellogg
Houston, Texas

Almost all of my work is on commission. The biggest consideration, for me at least, is the function of a piece. Even if that function is kind of made up (as it might be for a spec piece), I try to be as specific as possible. Whatever it is that that thing is supposed to be doing, I want it to do that one thing very, very well. From there, I try to figure out what the mood or the tone of the piece is. Friendly or formal? Masculine or feminine? I try to imagine the piece sitting in the client's house (or office, or church, or wherever). Is it smiling and waving, silently standing guard, or happy sitting quietly off to one side? I do a lot of writing at this point. Figuring out the tone of a piece will, more often than not, also determine what sort of wood I will end up using. I know some makers prefer to start with the wood: "I have this piece of walnut that just needs to be a cabinet..." But to me that feels too open-ended. It feels like floating in space.

Once those three things—function, tone, and wood— are more or less worked out, everything else starts to fall into place. I will generally build a full-scale mockup (or two, or three...) out of poplar and cardboard and hot-glue to get a sense of a piece's volume, or if there are going to be any parts that look like they might be trouble down the road. From there, if need be (say for a chair), I will make a full set of dimensioned drawings. After that, it's off to the races.

Game Chairs, 2014, cocobolo, wool felt upholstery, poplar, milk paint, mohair upholstery, 34" h x 18" w x 18" seat height. *Photo by Clark Kellogg*

Bridge Table, 2014, padauk, shop-sawn padauk veneer, shop-made brass hardware, 31" h x 40" square. *Photo by Clark Kellogg*

Justin King and Paula King

Beacon, New York

Rexhill brings time-honored quality to contemporary designs. Founders Justin and Paula King are a husband-and-wife team who are passionate about the value of making furniture by hand. They are proud to join the ranks of Americans reclaiming traditional craftsmanship.

Each piece of wood is hand-selected for its look and feel for a project and they prefer finishes that enhance its natural beauty. All of Rexhill's furniture and accessories are made in Beacon, New York, the heart of the Hudson Valley.

Phaedra Nighstand, 2013, walnut with parchment, 28" h x 18.5" w x 17" d. Photo by Liam Goodman Photography

#22 Lamp, 2014, walnut and linen, 22.5"h x 12" diam. *Photo by Liam Goodman Photography*

John Kirschenbaum
Seattle, Washington

My approach to furniture design is to first address fun. Over many years of designing, building, and learning from mistakes, the concept that form follows function has always made sense to me. It has actually liberated me from imitating other solutions and furniture styles. Function addresses not only mechanical aspects but also hand and eye appeal. An ugly piece isn't apt to be used as much no matter how well it functions mechanically. Yet, a pretty piece of wood is just that. I try to use the characteristics of the wood to complement the design rather than rely on its beauty alone. My design ideas come from a variety of sources: some from nature, some from art or architecture, and some from a strange corner of my imagination. I have fun building furniture and hope that anyone using my work will share that joy.

Dining Set with Six Chairs, sapelle, 74" x 42" x 29". *Exhibited in association with FS14 at the Northwest Woodworkers Gallery, Seattle.*

relevance: finding a context

STEPHEN HOGBIN

Relevance: "the relation of something to the matter at hand." That is a great definition for art, craft, and design, and has been a useful guide for me. Another meaning is "applicability to social issues" and that suggests being fully engaged within the context of community. Applicability is a good word made up of apply and ability. Imagining a relevant applicable future is fraught with problems. A useful way of understanding this concept is to look at a story from the past.

My great grandfather was a carver in cathedrals and a furniture maker. He lived in London, England. At that time, cities were having huge problems with horse manure. This problem was never talked about in the stories of his life. I became aware of it through Eric Morris who points out in his urban planners masters thesis.

> The situation seemed dire. In 1894, the *Times of London* estimated that by 1950 every street in the city would be buried nine feet deep in horse manure. One New York prognosticator of the 1890s concluded that by 1930 the horse droppings would rise to Manhattan's third-story windows. A public health and sanitation crisis of almost unimaginable dimensions loomed.

In my family history, there are stories of the wars, but no mention of the environmental degradation or appalling pollution in my great grandfather's life. That led me to think about my youth. I was born during the Second World War. In the late 1940s and early 1950s the London smog from coal burning was killing people. I was not allowed to run around outside on smog days. Wearing a white shirt was impossible, as it was dirty within a couple of hours. Those were everyday occurrences that changed the way we behaved.

Things need to change, whether it is horse manure, smog from coal burning, using fossil fuels, or refuse left over from the consumer society. The future is difficult if not impossible to predict. We need to think about it or be buried in the pollution of our own making.

While I was preparing an exhibition for the Center for Art in Wood in Philadelphia and thinking about a presentation, I became hyper-aware of a cardboard box. These days recycling and re-purposing are essential. Rather than sending stuff to the landfill, I was tearing off labels so the cardboard box could be used again. The box had many labels fixed to it and while stripping the box of these labels I started to recollect my history. The work was to be shipped to Del Mano Gallery in Los Angeles. I am not sure which piece went, but probably this one.

At the Del Mano Gallery, the piece was repacked with other artists' works and sent to SOFA in Chicago for the American Association of Woodturners (AAW) exhibition. I lost track of where it went next; it could have been to Minneapolis and the Gallery of the AAW or back down to the Del Mano Gallery.

Eventually the box came back to me. It was then reloaded for the *Pattern from Process* exhibition at the David Kaye Gallery in Toronto for a solo exhibition of work inspired by my new book *Hogbin on Woodturning*.

The David Kaye Gallery represents me in Canada. While that exhibition was on, the box returned and was repacked again for the *Wood and Water* exhibition at the Bruce Museum and Cultural Centre. That was an exhibition also presenting the work from my book.

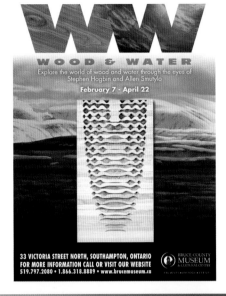

The *Pop–up* exhibition for the Center for Art in Wood was the next venue. Getting ready for the exhibition involved not only preparing the work, but also preparing the packaging.

In many ways, the box is a performance piece about recycling or re-purposing. Remember one of the meanings for relevance is "applicability to social issues." Re-purposing the box each time is being relevant. Each object gets a special wrap. The tissue paper was wearing out from the previous moves, so the flannelette cloth was selected as the next wrapper. The cloth is a better long-range solution. The soft white cloth soaks up the damp if it gets through the plastic bag wrap and is a cushion. The plan for the *Pop–up* exhibition was to travel to many new locations, which entails many packings and unpackings and repackings. Selecting the appropriate material was for me as important as making the work itself. This cardboard box keeps finding new places, and that is a satisfactory outcome.

The relevance of the cardboard box story is that the everyday objects are terribly important for today and tomorrow. It is relevant to the individual life of the maker, the user, and the viewer. There is nothing pretentious about this; it's just the right thing to do. Craft is about essential processes that enrich our lives and the lives of others. It represents the intentional life of the maker where the values work together and seamlessly.

What I have been describing is the gallery artist's experience, but not every maker will work this way.

There are four distinct ways of entering or approaching the furniture domain:

- Gallery artist
- Artisan producer
- Bespoke maker
- Educator demonstrator

These practices may be in combination, but, most likely, the maker becomes known within one of these fields. Education in the domain may not help establish a clear alternate way forward. Presenting clear options to the student is the better approach that not every instructor can offer. I will talk about each approach specifically.

The **gallery artist** is what I was describing in the cardboard box story, and it represents a typical engagement with organizations, galleries, and museums. It is a given that the work has to be good technically and aesthetically. Importantly, whatever is made has to work for the organization or end user. As soon as you step out of the studio workshop, a symbiotic relationship is entered. Put yourself in the other's shoes. Professional courtesy and being fully engaged is the only acceptable way forward. The field is highly competitive. Go to the opening of exhibitions. Talk to the gallery directors and museum curators. They are your allies. Their existence depends on artists and makers who are on top of their game. Not necessarily at the top of the domain, just on top of their own activity. If you think of this as a community of people that you are part of, then also connect with the collectors, journalists, and scholars. What I have described briefly as the gallery artist's activity surrounds the actual making. Put bluntly, it is not enough to just make good work.

When working with galleries and museums there is often a criteria or set of expectations that have to be fulfilled. Seldom will the organization come to you, saying they want to show your work. More likely, at least at the beginning, it is necessary to enter competitions to get your name and work out there. To illustrate, while writing this piece an email message came through from Craft Ontario. They were requesting submissions for exhibition. There were criteria that went like this:

Alignment with the Craft Ontario Exhibitions "Vision/Mission/Mandate"
- Demonstrates excellence
- Explores a new area of investigation and/or is inter-disciplinary
- Addresses historical context and/or tradition through contemporary work
- Provides an innovative approach and incites dialogue
- Promotes intercultural understanding

Establishing how well something works means it needs a criteria. The work is always assessed against some expectation. The solutions have to be relevant to a context. The viewer will measure how well it works against, for example "demonstrates excellence" or "promotes intercultural understanding."

The gallery artist must be able to respond to others' criteria as well as their own and look for a gallery that has the same values. If the gallery owner does not understand what you are doing, then you have real problems. The "artist statement" becomes an essential tool, not only for you, but also for the gallery and, ultimately, the purchaser. A simple, clear paragraph needs to represent you and your work. If you are not a great writer, get help. That's what I do.

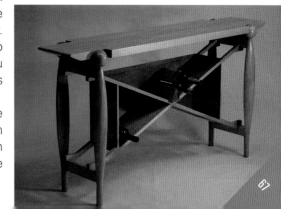

The **bespoke maker** has some similarities to the gallery artists, in that they will show their work in exhibitions occasionally. Usually, the bespoke maker will live in a community that's bigger than a village and smaller than a major urban center. The community is not just professionals from the domain, but people in a neighborhood who need something special to be made. The bespoke maker becomes known for certain things. It may include a particular aesthetic, but more likely it is the quality of workmanship, delivery on the agreed time, and a price that is reasonable and compatible with the trades. Most important for the maker is a reputation for integrity, that is, for process that is fully integrated. Supplying a story about the work has huge value. This story can be told at dinner parties and get the word of mouth developing. Journalists will also find the story helpful as they prepare to write about you and your work. Most of my work comes from people I know or friends of someone with whom I have worked.

Clients of the bespoke maker might have a very clear idea of what they want. I find they usually come to me saying that they like my ideas and are looking for something they saw on my website or in an exhibition. They may ask me to copy something they have seen in a magazine. It is important to decide what you will do or what you will pass to the maker down the road, and to get it right. Working with the client is great pleasure, usually.

Bringing clarity to the design process for the client is essential. Constructing the piece is only a part of the process. Constructing a relationship is equally important. The client may not be sure what they want. It may be necessary to

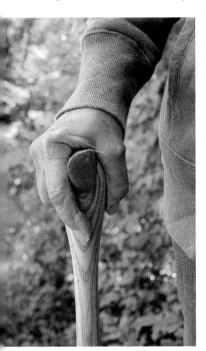

suggest that their idea won't work and that you have a better idea. If you don't like working with others, then being a bespoke maker is not a great way forward. If this is not an enjoyable process, then becoming a manufacturer or working in artisan production may be a better option.

I learned the hard way to get all the information up front and define the problem. When looking at the design proposal, I had a client say, "Oh, I wanted a French provincial design." Needless to say French provincial was not relevant to me or what I thought the context demanded. In that case, I suggested someone else, who will think that I have done them a real favor by passing the work along.

Clients range from immediate family, neighbors, people from the city, state, or province or occasionally internationally. The people you know are most likely to ask for specific problems to be solved. The problem solving starts at home. Take the walking cane as an example.

It was made for my partner. After much deliberation for this talk I selected the walking cane to talk about. It's so relevant; the selected cane is not on display in an exhibition. It is in play, being used every day. I like that when it's on display it's out of play. The play or story goes like this:

On a cold February morning, Margaret, my partner, was going to work. There was a very thin layer of powdery snow on black ice. Margaret slipped as she tried to cross the road breaking her ankle in several places. For a couple months she was in a wheelchair and then the cane became an essential object. I made a couple of canes. The first is ergonomically correct and fits her hand perfectly. That's the one shown here. The second cane was the production model quick to make with a generalized handle to fit the average-

size hand. Margaret prefers the custom-turned and carved solution with the comfortable fit to her hand.

This is the story of an everyday object that is indispensable, with extreme relevance, and it carries meanings of compassion and caring for the other. In my new book, I tell the story of each object. The object has a subject and a context. I have found it useful to evaluate my work through thinking about self, subject, object, and context.

The manufacturer or **artisan producer** is about making multiples of the same object. Most manufacturers have a range of products and one will sell better than another. There are three fundamental aspects to being in production. One, it's important to have a technical bent for efficient means through jigging, along with inventory control and a willingness to do it again and again. Two, being familiar with the new technologies is essential. The third is the ability to understand market trends and know the retailers who will represent the brand of objects. In addition, being

close to the market will cut down on shipping expenses. I find it challenging to sell one, let alone a batch of ten or a hundred.

I have had great success with salad servers and cutting boards, but when it comes to furniture, bespoke is a better approach for me.

A different temperament produces "one-offs" compared to production pieces. They both require problem-solving skills that are technical and aesthetic. It's more the human interaction with clients or retail buyers that needs different approaches. With the client, it becomes a discussion of personal needs and wants. The client, you hope, will be interested in your evolving style and there is a symbiotic relationship through a back and forth. It is a dance—a waltz with some, and a tango with others. The retail buyer will talk about trends, price point, and speed of delivery. It's less romantic and more of a hard-nose analysis of what's hot or

what's not. The magazines will push a particular color or look. We have just gone through or are going through, the exposed wain edge in table tops. There are some manufacturers who will lead the trends and the magazines will popularize the product. I find it all rather fickle, but others enjoy the challenge of figuring what's next.

The **demonstrator educator** starts out as a maker and then wants to share the knowledge. There is a full range of educational opportunities but universities require an MA to teach. The other equally important area is the front door of the studio, where talking with the public is a major opportunity to educate. They are equal opportunities but the pay scale may be different! It represents the next generation of makers and the next generation of buyers. The buyers need to be educated just as much as the makers. The last time I was in Australia, there were many makers who had a sales area where the public and maker would interact. In North America, we have the studio tours that are somewhat equivalent, although sporadic. I have found there is more time educating the public than there is making a sale. Between these two extremes there is a maker in my region with a tiny workshop selling turned spice mills. He also teaches classes with no more than three participants in the session. It's a highly effective business approach with a small, controlled product range sold mainly through craft fairs. The business is a combination of manufacturing in a small garage with occasional educational opportunities through a specific technique and product. It has a well defined, sharp focus.

Of the many teaching variations, the last maker educator I shall mention is the "circuit rider" of workshops and conferences. With a specific technique and an ability to demonstrate and talk about the process, it is possible to find colleges and clubs that will be interested in the demonstrator educator. Start with regional clubs and build out from there.

I can't emphasize enough the value of getting good at one thing first. Become known for a particular ability or product. Once people hear they may come looking for you or your work. Then build out from the particular to the general. It is a matter of seeing new relationships, connecting the dots, and grasping juxtapositions. It happens all the time in life; getting good at seeing relevance in the relationships is fundamental to any maker's practice. It is being mindful. Making the connection between the need and the outcome is something the pre-conscious can get very good at. Framing the problem really helps a good outcome. Like any journey, knowing where you want to go really helps. Get good at one thing and then, like the tree, branch out. Be radical—from your own roots. There is a slight danger of becoming too diverse and a jack-of-all-trades, but equally there is a danger in being too narrow and unable to find a large enough market. These days, with social networking, there is a better chance of success by being narrow in focus while presenting to the larger audience.

What makes one destination or piece of work better than another? Developing criteria and objectives is useful, if not essential. It's also understood as a "design brief." Educators will usually establish the guiding criteria for the student. On leaving education, the criteria will become yours, if you are working as an artist. If working with a client, the objectives are symbiotic and shared. If manufacturing, the market will push and pull in its unique fashion. Different temperaments will lean toward different approaches. Seldom are we brilliant in all ways.

And now, as I finish, let's think about the future and the idea of gridlock in our lives. I am a person from the country, while most people are living in North America's great urban centers, so the animal analogies may not work so well for you. But I think it's worth a try to see the other's point of view. Today's gridlock and pollution in the major centers is equivalent to the nineteenth century problem of horse manure. There is just too much of it. We each have to become part of the solution by not riding the horse to work, so to speak. Climate change is a huge problem we have inherited, and it's not going away soon. How relevant is your work in this context? How many more wacky objects does the environment need? Don't forget the cardboard box in which you will pack the relevant objects for others. These ideas are relevant; they count in the larger context and the way forward.

Another animal analogy I like goes like this: My daughter is a bee keeper and I occasionally help out. Bees are very interesting to work with and things need to be set up right. It is vital for colony survival. Making a context in which the bees will thrive is essential or they will fly away. In your practice as a maker, if things are not set up right, the bees and all the honey they represent will fly away. So you can see, horse manure—a huge problem. A well run bee hive—lots of honey.

Stephen Hogbin, a Canadian, graduated from the Royal College of Art in London, England. He started work as a studio artist in 1970 and was elected to The Royal Canadian Academy in 1983. He received the Queen Elizabeth II Diamond Jubilee Medal in 2012. Stephen exhibits widely in North America and beyond. He has had 36 solo exhibitions and over 200 group exhibitions in Australia, Canada, Europe, Japan, Korea, Russia and the U.S.

SUGGESTED READING:

Alan Bowness, gallery artist. *The Conditions of Success: How the Modern Artist Rises to Fame.* Thames and Hudson, London 1989. *A succinct text on the steps to take in becoming a successful artist.*

Douglas Harper, bespoke maker. *Working Knowledge: Skill and Community in a Small Shop.* University of Chicago Press, Chicago 1987. *The realities of working as a craftsperson in a community.*

Tony Fry, manufacturer. *Design Futuring: Sustainability, Ethics and New Practice.* Berg, Oxford International Publishers, Oxford, 2009. *The responsibilities to the future of the planet through "redirective practice."*

Bob Wiele, demonstrator/educator. *Smart for Life: Powerful Techniques for Achieving Personal Success and High Performance.* Fearless Diamond Press, One Smart World, Collingwood 2003. *Education must encourage creativity or it fails the future.*

David Knopp
Towson, Maryland

David Knopp has explored the aesthetic qualities of line for many years, first with life drawings, then with sculpture. A single line can express gesture and movement, direction and depth on a flat surface. Knopp made his first sculptures with plywood and was surprised to discover the linear strata inherent in the medium. Carving laminated blocks of the wood, Knopp creates flowing, liquid lines that engage the senses as the eye travels over the complicated contours of his objects.

The artist prefers an intuitive process, viewing the collaboration between ideas and materials central to his creative output. His creations start with a vision and a rough sketch. There are no defined templates or 3-D models or software used. His pieces are functional, but he tends to focus on the aesthetic qualities rather than design principles. Every finished piece is one-of-a-kind. The constant changes that occur as he works keep the work alive as it morphs into his interpretation. The process is paramount.

Phoenix (light), 2013, birch plywood, stack laminated and carved, 84" h x 48" w x 50" d. *Photo by David Knopp*

Sam Ladwig
Oklahoma City, Oklahoma

I was a professional musician, video producer, hi-tech project manager, graphic designer, and even an ice sculptor before focusing my creative energy on furniture design and fabrication. I recently received my MFA in furniture design from the Herron School of Art and Design in Indianapolis, but I currently live and work in Oklahoma City.

My furniture designs tend to follow modernist ideals, which, when viewed in isolation, lead to a minimalist and perhaps even cold aesthetic. However, my guiding principle is to always consider the pieces in context—including all of the additional visual information inherent in any space. When the pieces are placed in a more complex environment, I find that they provide formal stability while simultaneously generating interest. These images, staged and photographed by Chris and Deanne at Flux Gallery, capture the essence of that goal. As more complex and even aesthetically contradictory forms are added, the ability of the work to quietly and subtly ground the scene becomes more apparent. By simply changing accessories, you change the entire tone of a space. And to me, this is the sign that the piece is successful.

U-Line Console Table, 2014, white oak, laminated plywood, and powder coated steel, 25.75" h x 47" w x 14.125" d. *Photo by Chris Hansen and Deanne Roth*

Y-Line Sofa Table, 2014, white oak and stainless steel, 28" h x 60" w x 12.5" d. *Photo by Chris Hansen and Deanne Roth*

Mark Levin
Albuquerque, New Mexico

Woodworking has been my alcohol of choice. I've ridden it to the top and been dragged under by the undertow. I've never had any academic or philosophical discourse to wrap my work in; it rings false when I hear or read such artistic blathering. I build furniture because I love the process, from the first sketch to the sanding.

My work centers on nature's small wonders: leaves, flowers, fruit, seashells, nuts, etc. Mountains and oceans overwhelm, I don't have a chance. An apple or walnut I can grasp in my hand—there's that physical and visceral intimacy. They're perfect: shape, texture, color. Damn!

When I complete a piece and think that it's pretty good and I'm equally good, I get taken down fast the next time I see a flower or a leaf rustling in the breeze. I realize the best I can do is match mother nature, but rarely outpace her. On those days I do come up even with her, I'm as happy as a kid with an ice cream cone.

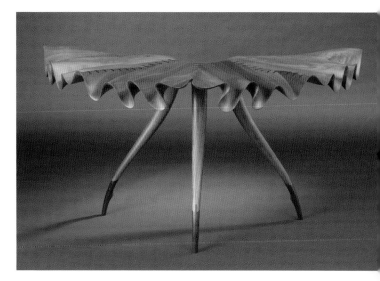

Vivaldi Leaf Hall Table, 2011, walnut, wenge, 30" x 55" x 25". *Photo by Margot Geist*

Pair of Apple Side Tables, 2013, curly birch, 18" x 26" x 33" each. *Photo by Margot Geist*

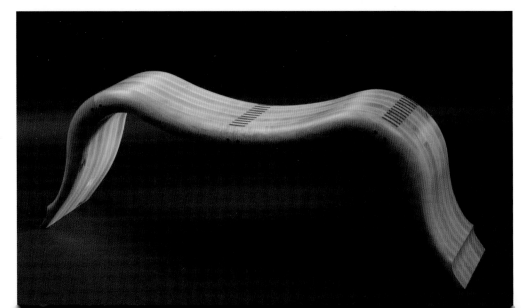

Ballerina Solo Bench, 2011, maple, bubinga, 19" x 58" x 12". *Photo by Margot Geist*

Aled Lewis
Rockport, Maine

Aled Lewis has been designing and making furniture for over thirty-five years. He makes special, useful, and beautiful pieces of furniture that resolve a design brief elegantly and skillfully, combining a functional requirement with an aesthetically pleasing resolution.

Lewis is the lead instructor of the nine-month comprehensive course at the Center for Furniture Craftsmanship in Rockport, Maine. He divides his time between Maine and his native Wales, teaching, designing, and making furniture.

He produces work that spans a wide range of designs and styles. For each project, Lewis aims for logical, practical, and elegant design solutions. For each piece, the technical resolutions are sound and appropriate, based on a thorough understanding of the materials and construction. Attention to detail is paramount: the selection of the finest timber, most suitable complementary materials, and best manufacturing techniques guarantee a product at the highest standards.

Lewis is a Fellow of the Royal Society of Arts, a Freeman on the Worshipful Company of Furniture Makers, and a member of The Furniture Society. He exhibits work in London and New York and his furniture is in private collections in both the U.K. and U.S.

Idris Hall Stand, 2012, oak and bloodwood, 84" x 49" x 17". *Photos by Chris Pinchbeck*

En Pointe Side Table, 2010, bleached ash and bloodwood, 33" x 52" x 14". *Photos by Jim Dugan*

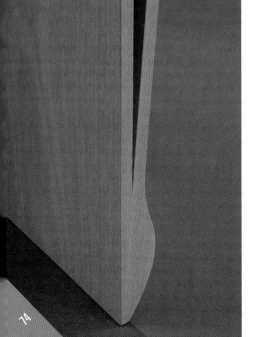

74

Chen Li
San Francisco, California

Chen Li graduated from Beijing Forestry University in 2010, where he received a BS in wood science and technology (furniture design and manufacturing). In 2013, he received an MFA in woodworking and furniture design at the Rochester Institute of Technology.

During his attendance at RIT, Li worked as a graduate assistant. In 2012, Li's work was a part of the exhibition entitled *The Creative Process*, which was held at Gallery r in New York. In 2013, he held his thesis exhibition at the Bevier Gallery, New York.

In 2013, Li joined San Francisco Woodshop as apprentice and now works with John Sheridan.

Chair, 2012, maple, 20" l x 17" w x 28" h (seat height, 18").

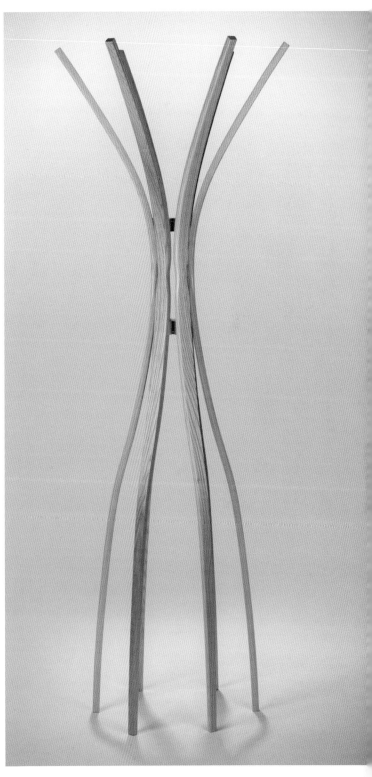

Blossom Coat Rack, 2011, ash, 72" h x 18" w x 18" d.

Wayne Liang

Stool, veneer, 24" x 12" x 12". *2014 Faculty Selects Winner, Exhibited at FS14, the Port Townsend Chapel.*

Brett Lundy
Toronto, Ontario, Canada

After studying Art History at the University of Toronto, Brett Lundy pursued a career in jewelry making before discovering the craft of furniture design and construction. An intensive course with wood guru Michael Fortune reinforced Lundy's passion for building studio furniture. He founded Merganzer Furniture in Toronto, where he designs and builds one-of-a-kind custom pieces and limited run studio furniture in the city's west end.

Lundy describes his work as "furniture your grandchildren will use." His designs are constantly evolving to explore the boundaries of material and techniques to find the perfect balance of form and function. Inspiration from nature can be seen in the countless carvings and organic curves that appear in these elegant and contemporary pieces.

John G. Marckworth
Port Townsend, Washington

John Marckworth is a custom woodworker and woodworking educator in Port Townsend, Washington. In 2010, Marckworth retired his business—Marckworth Specialty Woodworking— to devote his time and energies to the Port Townsend School of Woodworking, which he co-founded with Jim Tolpin and Tim Lawson in 2007. He continues to occasionally produce furniture on commission or a whim.

I have worked as a carpenter, cabinetmaker, and furniture maker for over thirty years. Since all my projects are custom, I have created work of many different types and styles, always seeking to stretch artistic boundaries while remaining true to the goals of design integrity and meticulous craftsmanship.

Dam Console, 2012, curly maple 35" h x 32.5" w x 13.25" d. *Photos by Brett Lundy*

Wave Table, 2012, hand-carved solid walnut, 15" h x 38" w x 24" d. *Photos by Brett Lundy*

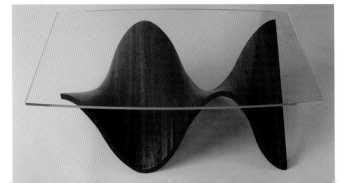

Built-in Entertainment Center, 2009, Douglas fir and Douglas fir plywood with bloodwood inlay, touch latches, 94" h x 72" w x 24" d. *Photo by John Marckworth*

Sarah Marriage

Hoboken, New Jersey

Sarah Marriage is a maker of fine furniture and other wooden objects, based in Hoboken, New Jersey.

Drawing from her background in architecture, structural engineering, and fine woodworking, Marriage's work explores both the whimsy and gravity of the objects in our lives. Using responsibly harvested timbers, Marriage designs and builds pieces by applying historical mechanical solutions to modern forms that thoughtfully address the rituals of daily life. The craft and design publication *Handful of Salt* described Marriage's work as, "wickedly seductive, in a very proper way."

Born in Tulsa, Oklahoma, and raised in Anchorage, Alaska, Marriage studied architecture at Princeton University and fine woodworking at The College of the Redwoods. Her work has shown at Dwell on Design in Los Angeles, Handmade/Mindmade in San Francisco, and Pritam & Eames Gallery in East Hampton, New York. She is also co-editor and co-founder of the online arts, literature, and craft quarterly *Works & Days*.

October Box, Pacific madrone, brass, silk, shellac, 3.75" x 10" x 14". *Exhibited at FS14, the Port Townsend Chapel.*

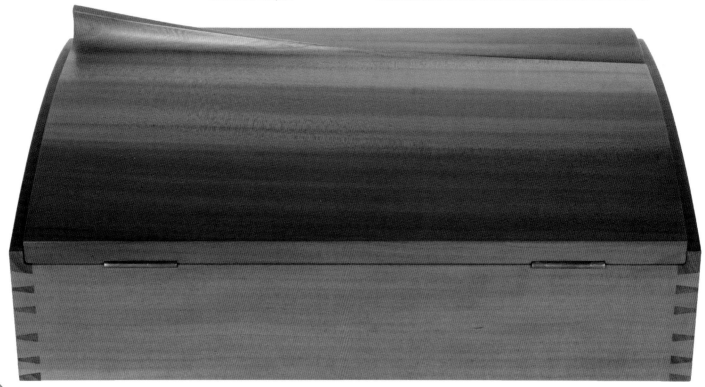

Chris Martin
Ames, Iowa

I recently lived and worked in Ghana, West Africa, where I served as a U.S. Peace Corps volunteer. To say that I was deeply affected by my experiences would be an understatement.

I found Ghana to be a country of amazing cultural diversity, ecological diversity, and diverse ways of thinking. It is a country filled with wonderful people and great potential, but it is also a country of great paradoxes and serious contradictions. My personal journey could also be described as disparate and contradictive. I felt as if I was being constantly jerked back and forth from deep frustration to profound jubilation.

Upon my return, I continued to develop work that portrayed the effect that living in Ghana has left upon me. This work is the embodiment of my personal reflections, and the processing of thoughts, and emotions that I continue to go through while I readjust to life back in America. I draw inspiration from the local tribal aesthetics to help express various issues. The work reflects various craft forms and pays homage to the traditional artisans. Through this work, I am projecting the concerns, frustrations, joys, and beauty I encountered on a daily basis, as well as the new perspective I have gained of my own culture.

Tribal Stool—Industrial Felt, 2013, waterjet cut industrial felt, 16" x 25" x 12".

CFS 4 & CFS 3, 2013, carbon fiber & bamboo, 4-legged: 29" x 17" x 13", 3-legged: 16" x 14" dia.

Prama Peewa, 2011, bur oak, English brown oak, gold leaf, trade beads, cloth, 67" x 23" x 18".

Sean Mckenzie
St. Petersburg, Florida

Sean Mckenzie began woodworking at age fifteen, entering the small Baulines Craft Guild and working under legendary woodworker Art Espenet Carpenter. Mckenzie grew up in the Bay Area of San Francisco where his roots in watching and participating in the politics of small businesses and human rights were a daily affair.

The cabinet expresses the frustration many voters felt with both political parties and with the government's inability to help the majority of Americans and small businesses. *Cabinet for a Big Divide*, made of walnut and curly maple, is still meaningful, as issues divide us as they have for so many years.

Voting Booth: Cabinet for a Big Divide, 2012, walnut & curly maple, 70" h x 35.25" w x 11.25" d

James Mellick
Milford Center, Ohio

Half of my career has been spent professing my craft at the college level and half has been spent as a full-time artist in the art market.

My carved and assembled dogs are about more than the dog or a particular breed. This is just part of the layered content. They are allegorical or poetic expressions of how I see world events and human behavior. As "man's best friend" the dog is the "totem" animal of humankind. Layered in the carved constructions and the complexity of engineering, design, and craftsmanship are symbols that I intend to convey meaning. The narrative animal sculptures are parables, like illustrations before the story is written.

Occasionally, I will bring some function to the form of my wood sculptures to justify their taking up floor space and to validate my being a member of The Furniture Society.

I hope that the viewer of my sculpture experiences a unity of a significant idea, beautiful form, and exquisite craftsmanship—a craftsmanship that intimidates my post-modern, deconstructed art colleagues.

Bird Dog, 2003, cherry, birch, cast bronze and copper detail, 28" h x 53" w x 20" d. *Photos by James Mellick*

Allen Miesner
Richmond, California

There is a history of furniture making in my family. My two grandfathers made furniture: one owned a lumber mill and was fabricating furniture in Missouri, and the other designed and made chiropractic tables during the Depression. It was my great uncle Mike who had the most influence on me. Uncle Mike was a craftsman/carpenter; he let me use his workshop and taught me the basics. I learned a lot from him and others. When my uncle died at 90 years of age, I inherited his tools and purchased his house with its backyard shop!

Another influence in my life was the surrealist Czechoslovakian photographer Vilem Kriz, with whom I studied for many years. Vilem was a master of composition and our conversations about form and balance have helped me greatly. Applying aesthetics of photography to the function of furniture is an interesting mix.

I like working with a variety of materials, but it is usually wood or metal that I use. Those two materials don't always get along in the studio, but in the finished piece they are quite happy together. Recently 3-D printing has taken over a corner of the studio; not sure where that is going, but the brain cells are stimulated.

Hubcap Bench, 2012, afromosa wood, aluminum, 80" w x 20" d x 17" h.

Charles Mitchell
Port Angeles, Washington

Charles Mitchell is an artist who creates furniture that is a balance of function and aesthetics. Charles's inspiration heralds from his observations in nature as much as from his upbringing in a multigenerational wooden boat building family.

Raised in California, he was afforded a wide variety of inspirations to pull from, living close to the coast, which continues as a base of his creative character. Charles now resides in Washington, on the Olympic Peninsula where he has a large shop at home. Having honed his skills over a lengthy career, he continues to enjoy the opportunity to create new furniture and collaborate on installations with a host of clients, including individuals and designers.

Employing nearly lost techniques such as steam bending, laminating, and extensive hand tool work, Charles unites the finest materials to create artistic furniture poised for handing down to future generations. Compiling from the natural surroundings that wrap the West Coast, Charles's works span a vast array of ability including large, live-edge works and delicate, kinetic sculpture pieces.

River Bench, bay laurel and claro walnut, 18" x 17" x 57.25". *Exhibited at FS14, the Port Townsend Chapel.*

I Carry These People with Me Entry Hall Table, VG fir, African mahogany, copper boat nails, 57" x 13.5" x 27". *Exhibited in association with FS14 at the Northwest Woodworkers Gallery, Seattle.*

Hugh Montgomery
Bainbridge Island, Washington

I specialize in designing and building contemporary furniture that has been influenced by early American (Shaker and Craftsman) and European furniture (Scandinavian design). My designs reflect the lasting character of these traditional styles with a refined modern flair. Many of my designs have repeating elements and play with the balance between the gracefulness of a curve and the rigidity of a straight line. I use traditional building methods, such as mortise-and-tenon joinery, veneering, and bent wood processes. The finest commercial veneers, solid wood, and re-sawn veneers are often incorporated into my furniture designs to achieve a consistent color match or to take advantage of a figured board. My approach to furniture making is a balance between traditional hand skills and effective machine use.

I believe that a well-proportioned piece of furniture should capture the eye of the beholder from a distance and entice them to come closer and examine and touch the piece. I strive to build within these parameters and seek to draw attention to my furniture by enlivening traditional forms with subtle details such as beveled relief, delicate inlay, curved and angled elements, tapered legs and contrasting woods. These finely executed details are what give my pieces their handcrafted appeal.

After graduating from Middlebury College in Vermont, I built houses in coastal Maine and enrolled in the Boston Architectural Center (BAC), where I learned design and drafting techniques that I still use in my work today. I moved to Seattle in 1990 and began working in a cabinetmaking shop. Seeking to refine my woodworking skills, I apprenticed with a furniture maker in a co-op shop and took furniture making classes, including a class taught by renowned furniture maker Michael Fortune.

Since 1995, I have been on Bainbridge Island building furniture and custom cabinets in my home-based shop.

Essential Table, madrone & madrone burl veneer, 17" d x 23" h. *Exhibited in association with FS14 at the Northwest Woodworkers Gallery, Seattle.*

Rangeley Morton
Chelmsford, Massachusetts

Rangeley Morton explores mobile design through the creation of flat-pack furniture for modern living. Furnishings are designed with a focus on collapsible ingenuity and the study of infra-structural systems. Work is fabricated in three dimensions through a combination of traditional handcraft and digital production. His furniture evokes a playful curiosity that is both functional and whimsical.

While growing up, Morton was fascinated with assembling, modifying, and disassembling. His desire to make furniture was born out of this inherent impulse to play. Morton graduated with a BFA in woodworking and furniture design from Maine College of Art. He went on to be junior artist in residence at San Diego State University in the graduate program. A 2014 Windgate Fellowship recipient, Morton is creating a benchtop prototyping studio made up of transportable tools to continue his work.

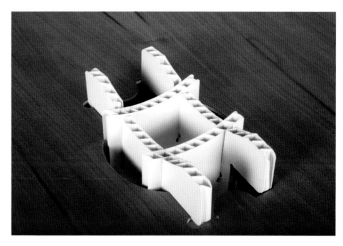

Knox Table, plastic, plywood, solid wood, 48" x 48" x 30". 2014 Faculty Selects Winner, *Exhibited at FS14, the Port Townsend Chapel.*

Eric Nation
Seattle, Washington

As a child, I was immersed in a can-do environment. My maternal grandfather was a highly respected landscape painter, engineer, and part-time rancher. My father built our house, as did his father before him. It was always assumed that if something had to be done, you did it yourself.

Inspired by such an impressive collection of skilled, motivated people, I found myself instinctively drawn to the process of making, using whatever tools and materials were at hand. Architecture and the methods and materials of construction became my early focus. The process of design/build gave me immediacy and control over how my ideas were interpreted. It also gave me the flexibility to alter work as it progressed. Finding myself limited by the scale and timeframes of architecture, I began to pursue furniture. Furniture provided many of the same challenges of structure, function, and space that I had faced in architecture, yet I could work through ideas much faster and affordably.

The work created since 2005 is an intentional movement away from the more direct architectural influences of earlier works that began in 1988. These newer pieces walk a fine line between sculpture and functional furniture. They increasingly incorporate a narrative gesture that draws the viewer into a dialog beyond the physical interaction required by a functional object.

Home Sweet Home, 2013, mixed media, 65" x 10" x 12". *Photos by Russell Johnson*

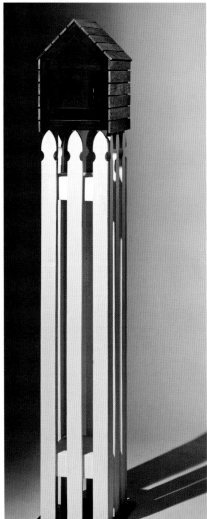

Span II, 2005, glazed ceramic, oak, basswood, maple, 16" x 82" x 22". *Photo by Larry Stanley*

Bart Niswonger
Worthington, Massachusetts

I design and build furniture that explores the balanced interaction of form and surface; invites both visual and tactile interaction; and references tradition while exploiting modern techniques.

Wall Cabinet (Translucent Blue Doors), 2012, ash, cast urethane, paint, 22" x 22" x 6".

Red & Yellow Cabinet on Stand, 2012, Ash, cherry, paint, cast urethane, 33" x 16" x 41".

James R. Oleson
Chapel Hill, North Carolina

In designing furniture, I prefer a spare and elegant aesthetic that incorporates relatively few decorative accents but does emphasize curves in three dimensions. I use woods that have intrinsic beauty of color and grain to reinforce the design concept. With each piece, I enjoy exploring the use of a new material, technique, or design, and this has enabled me to continually develop and expand my skills.

I strive to create works displaying a high level of craftsmanship that also embody the fundamental principles of art: harmony, rhythm, and balance.

Bristlecone Pine Marquetry Cabinet, 2014, sapele hardwood and a variety of veneers, 66" h x 27" w x 13.25" d. *Photo by J.R. Oleson*

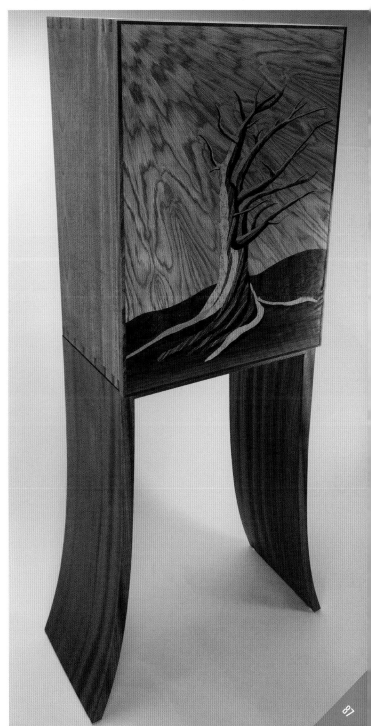

Marcus Papay
Encinita, California

Marcus Papay is a furniture designer working from his studio shop in San Diego, California. Marcus creates unique works that incorporate the characteristics of furniture design from both the past and the present. His individual style brings in modern aesthetics with processes that embrace traditional design and the handmade.

Papay's work subtly evokes an interpretation of recognizable design that represents the Southern California lifestyle while insisting on a quality that counters the disposable mentality of product design. All elements are designed using 3-D modeling programs to be made in a small shop where production quantity does not interfere with creativity.

Today, the studio of Papay Designs is focusing on new lighting fixtures that explore the flexibility of working without the confines of the retail market. With intensions of developing a body of one-off sculptural lighting fixtures, Papay hopes to pay homage to the meaningful connection we have to the creative objects in our homes and public spaces.

Sinuous Floor Lamp, 2013, carbon fiber strands, epoxy, walnut, aluminum, light 60" x 24" x 24". *Photo by Barry Calhoun*

place as space

PETER KASPER

Long ago, explorers showed us that the world was round. In the intervening five hundred years, we have managed to shrink its scale drastically. Humanity's inventive nature now mixes people, ideas, and goods at a rate suitable to make Columbus's head explode.

When I tell a stranger, "I'm a studio furniture maker," I'm greeted with a puzzled look, so I quickly follow up with, "You know, fine wood furniture and cabinets." I then find myself fending off idyllic notions of age-old tools and techniques, noble traditions and dovetails... along with the absurd questions about injuries, long beards, and shop elves. The truth is, modern makers are in a much different landscape than a generation ago.

Telling a designer to "know their place" is pretty insensitive and implies a certain level of arrogance and ego. At best, the designer is reduced to being a small cog in a machine of engineers, builders, and most importantly, consumers. At worst, tempers rise, resentment brews, and design quality goes out the window.

However, rephrasing "know their place" as "empathize with your place" can inspire and inform the designer and maker. Creating studio furniture can be seen as the crossroad of place and time. The original location of the materials, the space where it is made, and the significance of where it will live can unite the past with the future.

As contemporary makers, we now exist in a marketplace—a global maker's renaissance— that is both fluid and dynamic. We have access to a more world- "globalier" workshop than ever before. Plug a phrase into Google® and you'll get more images than you can handle... many of which are, of course, useless. CAD drawings can fly through the Internet, designers can communicate worldwide in real time, and materials are processed and shipped at alarming speeds of turnaround. As our design world caters to a broader appeal and faces ever faster obsolescence as the audience moves on to the latest trend. In our expedited era, the necessity of defining our place is more important than ever.

Acknowledging our place shouldn't isolate us. In fact, it may provide a boost of inspiration. I am a fan of urban lumber, that is, lumber from trees growing in town. The logs are often scorned for commercial uses because of embedded metal, lower yield, inconsistent species, and lack of supply chain infrastructure. There is, however, a growing movement to keep these trees from becoming firewood.

The fact is that many species grown in urban environments offer exotic-looking woods at a lower price and with less harm to the ecosystem than most. The very defects that turn most individuals away can translate into stunning visual effects. A log with "defects" can tell some amazing stories of its time rooted in place; the knots, mineral streaks, and growth rings are journal entries over the course of its life.

Shelf made from sequential slabs of an urban ash log.

Trees are touted for the ecological benefits they give while they are living: shade, habitat, windbreak, and more. A tree provides these blessings while spending its whole life planted in one spot, dug into place through its roots, and not moving until its dying day. When that day comes and it is reduced to a log, the tree begins a long journey from sawmill to workshop, with stops at kiln processors, warehouses, and wholesalers. Along the way it is graded, steamed, and reshuffled into a large, homogenous pile of boards with little attention paid to the character that distinguishes one stick from the next. The hitchhiking log racks up exhaust fumes and its price is marked up as it moves from middleman to middleman.

When the logs are kept local, the benefits the tree once gave to its surroundings can continue in new and beautiful forms. In the hands of a creative maker, the tree's life is perpetuated, and it is reincarnated into a pleasing, useful new phase of existence.

In recent years, the local foods movement has done a great job of popularizing the farm-to-table loop as a way of improving quality, cutting down on shipping costs, and creating cooperative relationships between the growers and their customers. In the same way, by highlighting the origin of the tree, the maker helps the consumer invest in the community and brings a value to the finished piece with which the consumer can identify. The advantage of studio furniture is that it is experienced in person, and as it is encountered, a one-to-one relationship forms. The item is neither mass-produced, nor mass-consumed. The smaller loop from design to consumer offers a chance to reduce overhead costs and highlight the material as an art form.

Desk made from locally sawn hickory and walnut. The hickory was cut to make way for a parking lot and was headed for firewood when the author snagged it.

Kelly Parker
Parkville, Missouri

Kelly Parker, born in Phoenix, Arizona, in 1967, is a designer and maker of contemporary studio furniture and sculpture. After graduating with a degree in biochemistry, she worked in the corporate world for eighteen years before taking a rather circuitous route into art. In 2009, she took the plunge, shucked the safety of the corporate world and decided to make her living as a woodworker. She has taken numerous design and technique classes at Anderson Ranch Arts Center and the Marc Adams School of Woodworking, where she is currently working on her Michael Fortune Fellowship.

Parker has a deep admiration and reverence for wood and loves creating beautiful, functional art with it. She designs and creates one-of-a-kind and limited production pieces in her studio in Parkville, Missouri, often incorporating other materials such as metal and glass.

Daisy, 2014, bamboo with caramelized vertical grain face and strand core, reclaimed walnut, aluminum dowel, aluminum inlay, 18" x 19" x 19". *Photo by Kelly A Parker*

Peter K Pestalozzi
Ely, Minnesota

I have been a furniture builder for thirty-nine years now. Over the past seven years, I have made a number of pieces that have been based on places and imagery from Lake Superior. While traveling on the lake, I use my camera to bring home images that inspire me. In working out the designs for the furniture pieces, I will distill these images and then incorporate these elements in the work.

Surf's up Rocker, 2012, walnut, black sheep skin, 48" t x 22" w x 42" d. *Photo by Peter K Pestalozzi*

Norman Pirollo
Ottawa, Ontario, Canada

Refined Edge Design brings forward a unique form of studio furniture incorporating contemporary and modern elements. As designer, Norman Pirollo, has acquired an education from contemporary artisans as well as a breadth of insight into both the visual and decorative arts. Through equal amounts of patience, attention to detail, and a keen sense of design, Pirollo creates striking studio furniture incorporating unique, contemporary designs. Applying accumulated skills and expertise, he pursues the design process from preliminary sketches to CAD drawings to making.

Pirollo selects the highest quality and most dramatically figured woods as components of his unique designs. Design, wood preparation, and finishing are a large part of his work and, therefore, he devotes considerable time to these stages. His work has been featured in books such as *Studio Furniture: Today's Leading Woodworkers*, *Wood Art Today 2*, and *500 Cabinets*, as well as in magazines like *Fine Woodworking*, *Woodwork*, *Ottawa Life*, *Ottawa Citizen*, *Panoram Italia*, *NICHE Magazine*, and other publications.

Chaotic Cabinet, 2012, ambrosia maple, maple, cocobolo, cherry, 56.5" h x 18.5" w x 13" d. *Photo by Linda Chenard*

Andrew Pitts

Heathsville, Virginia

I am a largely self-taught furniture maker and former naval officer with thirty-eight years of studio furniture experience. I built my workshop in the secluded forests of Northumberland County, Virginia, and have been designing and making furniture full time for nine years. My furniture has been featured in numerous exhibitions, garnering more than a dozen awards. I love to create furniture, relishing the freedom to transform wonderful woods into equally wonderful pieces that people can use. My furniture career has been a journey where new discoveries are an essential component; the artisan unlocks the wonders of the material, but the synergy of the client/artisan relationship can result in the finest designs.

Old Bridge Paschal Candle Stand, 2010, cherry, shellac, brass, 40" h x 11" w x 11" d.
Photo by Andrew Pitts

Dean Pulver
El Prado, New Mexico

Dean Pulver is a full-time furniture maker and sculptor working in Taos, New Mexico. He is primarily a woodworker who makes his living through one-of-a-kind works, private commissions, and limited production sales. He has taught at the Center for Furniture Craftsmanship, Penland School of Crafts, and Anderson Ranch Arts Center. His works are shown in galleries and museum exhibitions and collections nationally.

My hope is to create a beauty that is true and pure, and resonates in the mind inescapably. Seducing the senses through the opposition and balance of forms, textures, and content. To create pieces that are raw and honest and express the perfection in imperfection. Layered with reference to nature, culture, creativity, life and living, they are meant to be monuments to our existence.

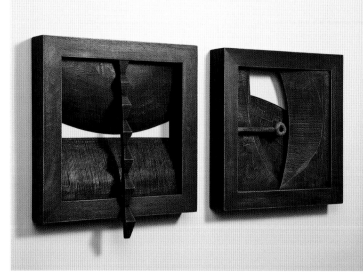

Parts of a Whole, 2009, dyed walnut, 18" x 38" x 4". *Photo by Dean Pulver*

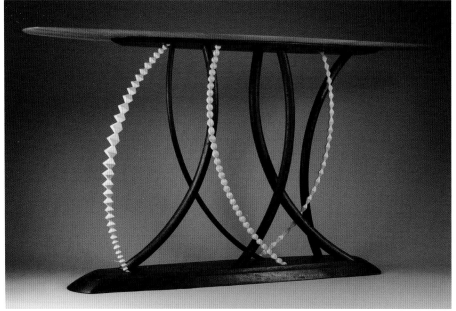

Crosswinds, 2013, sycamore, dyed and bleached walnut, 42" x 82" x 12.75". *Photo by Dean Pulver*

Michael Puryear
Shokan, New York

As a designer/studio furniture maker, the visual has always had a special resonance for me. The attraction of furniture, in particular, arose from my early awareness and appreciation of the clarity and directness of Shaker and Scandinavian design. Later the influence of Japanese, African, and other traditions were important. Individuals such as Wharton Escherick and James Krenov were models that inspired me.

The choice of wood as a medium is based in tradition, the nature of the technology, and its natural warmth and appeal to the hand. Not having any formal training, my furniture making skills are the result of reading and experimentation.

Wall-Hung Guitar Stand, 2012, mahogany, rosewood & maple, 24" w x 36" h x 12" d. *Photo by Michael Puryear*

Chess Bench, 2013, ash, poplar, cherry and milk paint, 80" w x 19" h x 20" d. *Photo by Michael Puryear*

Charles Radtke
Cedarburg, Wisconsin

When I set out create a piece of furniture, I begin with the intent to make something of lasting integrity. Using my knowledge of wood and its changing properties, I try to create a cohesive, well-crafted object. I work directly from design concept to execution, without making sketches. For me, something gets lost in trying to have the whole object figured out prior to building. Part of the journey of building is the unknown of the finished work. How is it going to end? It is this mystery that sustains my focus on a work from its conception to its completion.

I consider myself primarily a cabinetmaker. A cabinet is often the most curious and intriguing piece of furniture in a home. A cabinet holds things, like secrets. I'm drawn to that, as well as to the level of interaction required with a cabinet. You have to touch it, open it, manipulate it, and work with it. A cabinet also has many moving parts and thus requires a tremendous amount of detail work. Precise and well-executed detail work is a fundamental element in all of my furniture.

Over the years, I have had the opportunity to harvest much of the lumber I have used to create my furniture. This has been one of the most important and lasting influences on my work. It is a humbling process to watch as these large trees, which have stood for hundreds of years, finally die, and become lumber. I strive to assure their second life in a piece of furniture is as noble as their first.

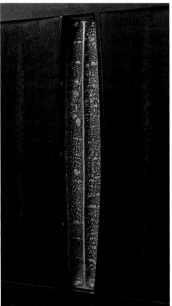

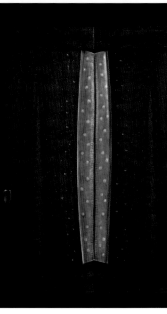

Box #154, 2014, holly, quilted aspen, anigré, French polish, 36" x 15" x 15". *Photo by Larry Sanders*

One Of One, 2012, gabon ebony, ebonized walnut, enameled fine silver, silver gilding, French polish, 46" x 16" x 16". *Photo by Larry Sanders*

Mike Randall
Victoria, British Columbia

Mike Randall, studio furniture maker and designer, works in a West Coast Modernist style. His love of clean lines and curved forms leads him to create beautiful and elegant pieces of furniture. He also frequently integrates metal into his designs to provide stunning contrast in both color and texture. He works closely with local artisans for all the metalwork and, where possible, uses locally sourced materials.

Randall is a graduate of the Fine Furniture Program at Camosun College. His "past lives" have included careers as a professional skipper of power and sail boats, and as a forester. These have provided him with an in-depth knowledge of the material from seed to finished product as well as a use of space that only comes from growing up around boats.

Randall was born and raised in the U.K., but came to Canada in 1999. He currently resides in Victoria, British Columbia, with his wife and two children.

Kurva is a Swedish word meaning bend, or arc, and the name of Randall's business, Kurva Design, reflects his love of both curved design and the Swedish country style of simple, clean, modern lines.

Kurva Chair, alder, ash, birch plywood, stainless steel, 32" x 25" x 23". *Exhibited at FS14, the Port Townsend Chapel.*

"Element" Series Bench, white oak and aluminum, 48" x 18" x 12". *Exhibited at FS14, the Port Townsend Chapel.*

Wave, alder and satin walnut veneer, 7" x 12" x 1". *Exhibited at FS14, the Port Townsend Chapel.*

Andrew Redington
Berlin, Wisconsin

As a craftsperson and maker of objects, I have a great passion for art and craft history. I have an interest in artwork that borrows from design. The adoption of design is employed for construction but also serves as a conduit for people to associate with it. I am interested in the idea of creating forms that build on the relationship we have with objects and the potential psychological impact they may have. The association that people have with objects is sometimes emotional in nature and sometimes the bond serves as an aid in memory.

In this series of work, if the viewer has ever closely inspected typical household furniture or even crawled underneath it as a child, they will easily recognize parts. Some parts are designed for utilitarian or structural purposes, while others have deliberate design aesthetics applied but the parts do not work independently for their original purpose. Changing the way the pieces are viewed and arranging them into a basic form and exposing other shapes, calls attention to them, while highlighting their role as an essential part. Through altering and subverting familiar forms, I expose the unseen and examine the significance.

For me, allegorically, the dissection and exposure of these parts, their rearrangement for inspection and placement to be a compulsory part of the whole, act as a metaphor for the obligatory in society.

50 Cubic cm of the Detritus from Changing Styles, upcycled furniture parts, 50 x 50 x 50 cm. *Exhibited at FS14, the Port Townsend Chapel.*

Cory Robinson
Indianapolis, Indiana

Cory Robinson is an artist, designer, and an associate professor of furniture design and Fine Arts chair at the Herron School of Art and Design. He has an MFA in furniture design from San Diego State University. Robinson has taught at Herron since the spring of 2003. In this time, he has continually sought ways to make his artwork reflect his interest in functional forms that speak with an artist's sensibility. The collective bodies of work move through many different explorations, representing material investigations, form investigations, the narrative qualities objects can hold, the formal vocabulary of design, and then back again to the joy found in making functional objects.

Robinson gravitates toward historic references found in furniture design itself; the language of the Shaker communities, early American furniture and the native Hoosier cabinets. In recent studio work, Robinson has relied heavily on traditional furniture-making techniques and language to arrive at finished works that blend new and old materials with new and proven design dialogues. Using reclaimed, aged material to contrast other elements within the design, put technology driven processes like CNC-cut acrylic alongside the traditional processes of using resins, wood, and steel in the creation of the form.

New Antique vol.2–bench, 2011, reclaimed barn widing, acrylic, 17" x 15" x 49". *Photo by Calen Charland*

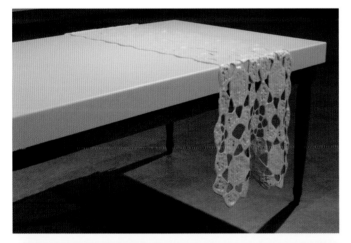

Forever After She is Gone, 2011, reclaimed barn siding, steel, lace, resin, paint, 17" x 22" x 38" each table. *Photo by Calen Charland*

Seth Rolland
Port Townsend, Washington

Seth Rolland is a custom furniture maker whose work is influenced by natural forms, Japanese and Danish aesthetics, and explorations of structure and balance. His materials strongly influence his work. Stone is used as mass to balance cantilevers and anchor structures. Wood is shaped to reflect the subtle and dramatic curves found in nature, or cut and bent, expanding it into sculptural and functional forms.

Seth produces custom commissions for clients, speculative pieces for shows, and semi production designs for museum stores and galleries across the country. He lives and works in Port Townsend, Washington.

Barstool, walnut, 18" x 18" x 41". *Exhibited in association with FS14 at the Northwest Woodworkers Gallery, Seattle.*

North Beach Hill Table, beech and stone, 32" x 61" x 15". *Exhibited at FS14, the Port Townsend Chapel.*

Wood Vase, cherry. *Exhibited at FS14, the Port Townsend Chapel.*

Hunter Roth
Norman, Oklahoma

Hunter Roth was born in New Orleans and raised mostly in Baton Rouge where he earned his BFA from Louisiana State University. He was hired shortly after graduating to manage the Design Shop, a woodshop lab for the College of Art & Design at LSU. During Roth's time at LSU, he also instructed furniture design classes as an adjunct professor. In January of 2011, Roth was hired to manage the Creating/Making Lab for the College of Architecture at the University of Oklahoma and to sporadically teach an advanced furniture design class. He is a multi-talented artist: a painter, drawer, sculptor, printmaker, furniture maker, digital fabricator and musician.

My artwork is often surreal, interactive, kinetic, colorful, and playful. I gather inspiration from my environment or a character in my imagination. My sculptures are like big toys or games, designed to be interactive with the audience or environment. I love to create for fun and function with found objects or materials I have on hand. Unique objects inspire me and give me direction as an artist. Often I will see an object or scrap piece of material and know instantly what I want to create from it. Its origin and characteristics inspire the content and encourage me to further its story.

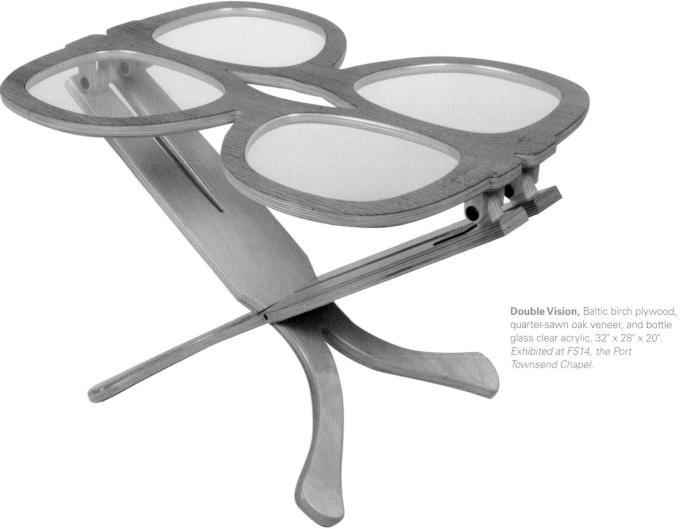

Double Vision, Baltic birch plywood, quarter-sawn oak veneer, and bottle glass clear acrylic, 32" x 28" x 20". *Exhibited at FS14, the Port Townsend Chapel.*

Maggie Sasso

St. Francis, Wisconsin

Maggie Sasso received her BFA from Murray State University in 2006 and her MFA from the University of Wisconsin–Madison in 2010. She has taught at UW–Madison, Oregon College of Art and Craft, and currently at the Milwaukee Institute of Art and Design.

She is serving on the Board of Trustees of The Furniture Society and did so once before as the Student Representative in 2004-05. Sasso works collaboratively on projects, such as the grant-funded Mobile Museum of Material Culture, which was featured in the documentary "Blink Again," an installation for the Madison Children's Museum, and at collaborative events like the Emma International Collaboration and the Hawaii Artist Collaboration. Sasso has created numerous rigorously conceptual bodies of work that reflect her formal craft education.

Sasso has the uncanny ability to find double-entendre in the least likely of places. Her work examines the language and history of flags, maps, and maritime culture. By interrogating specific objects, unpacking and twisting their meanings back on themselves, she comes to discover the unique stories they each hold, and the ways in which they succeed and fail in imparting the stories to us. In a process of radical transformation, they become new. Bosun's Chair is based on a historical form, which Sasso has transformed into a theatrical and comically dysfunctional rescue device that speaks not only to her personal narrative, but also to the cultural absurdities and conventions that we all face.

Bosun's Chair, mixed media, 36" x 36" x 8". *Exhibited at FS14, the Port Townsend Chapel.*

Anelise Schroeder
Brooklyn, New York

Anelise Schroeder is a furniture designer currently living in Brooklyn, NY. She is a recent graduate of the Rhode Island School of Design, where she explored a lifelong interest in interactive objects. Anelise's work often draws from her Norwegian heritage to create something unexpected from traditional craftwork. Her pieces reflect a hands-on and experimental approach, always with a focus on exploring new materials and processes.

Setesdal Bench, steel, wool, yarn, 18" x 36" x 18". 2014 Faculty Selects Winner, *Exhibited at FS14, the Port Townsend Chapel.*

Bruce M. Schuettinger
New Market, Maryland

Bruce M. Schuettinger graduated with honors in art and bachelor of science degree with a fine arts major. He is the owner and principal conservator of Schuettinger Conservation Services, Inc. and for over 30 years has been an author and lecturer about historical furniture from the classical societies of Egypt, Greece, and Rome to present day Artist Craftsman movement. He is uniquely positioned to understand the work and design principles from several thousand years. This knowledge, combined with crafts skill honed from his years at the bench working with wood and re-creating all forms of turned, carved, inlayed, painted, gilded elements, informs his creative work at his Art in Furniture by Schuettinger studio in New Market.

Abstract Organic Expressionism 1, 2, 3 Coffee Table with Matching Left and Right End Tables, 2014, naturally downed solid walnut and veneers, coffee table 61" x 22" x 20", end tables 30" x 22¼" x 24".

Jay T. Scott
Olympia, Washington

I watch my work evolve, learning to be patient. I am working to express myself in a subtle way, in a simple form. I look for beauty in a subtle curve, in line and proportion. I look to the functional objects in our lives and make them in an artful way.

I compose my designs from many different styles of furniture and architecture. From other art forms, bodies, the curve in a blade of grass. I am infatuated with the shape and gesture of the hand, and with what it is able to create.

It is important to me to be sensitive to the material itself, allowing the material to have a voice in the desire to create.

My work is a reflection on how we live and how we respond to objects. It reflects my practice of working the way we love, pursuing excellence, and attending to the details and possibilities of each piece.

My work is also a record of the passing of time. Each piece grows from an idea to an object and in the process, I take time to observe and see the opportunities in the work. The objects I make then become part of another person's life and story. Watching them age, the wood changes color, handles are polished by fingers, the patina of use, of life.

Owl Cabinet, big leaf maple, yellow cedar, leather, bronze hardware, 56.5" x 18" x 35". *Exhibited in association with FS14 at the Northwest Woodworkers Gallery, Seattle.*

Alfred Sharp
Woodbury, Tennessee

After a half-hearted attempt at a law degree, Alf Sharp discovered his true vocation in fine furniture making. Thirty-five years later he's still at it with as much enthusiasm as at the beginning. Almost all work is done on a custom commission basis, in close collaboration with clients and their designers.

Specializing in eighteenth- and nineteenth-century American and European design, Sharp also enjoys Beidermeier, Art Deco, Chinese, and contemporary design. His own original work has, most often, at least a toe-hold in tradition.

Sharp has pieces in historical homes and museums throughout the U.S., as well as in fine private homes nationally. He is the recipient of the 2008 Cartouche award from The Society of American Period Furniture Makers. He is past president of The Furniture Society. When not absorbed in the woodshop or playing with his grandchildren, he enjoys restoring and driving classic British sports cars.

Lady's Writing Desk, 2009, satinwood, rosewood, 72" h x 18" d x 40" w. *Photo by John Lucas*

Maloof-esque Rocking Chair, 2012, walnut, maple, cherry, 43" h x 40" d x 26" w.

John Sheridan

Chen Li, assisting
San Francisco, California

Our work is ongoing, project-focused studio furniture based on the Bauhaus/Black Mountain College model. The direction is from theory and sketch to prototypes and final pieces. We begin with a repetitive processing of six to eight items to strengthen a foundation of competency. We begin by making sanding blocks and safety push sticks, moving on to the wedged mortise-and-tenon and dovetail, classic and historically important woodworking joints. From there we progress to tool trays and step stools. Finally, we make small tables, benches, or other objects. New techniques such as the Lamello biscuit and Festool tenon are used. We experience what "sharp" is in the world of tools by preparing our chisels.

The challenges are continuous as we consider concepts, ideas and historical references for our furniture. The joinery (the connecting of pieces of wood) is hand and machine cut and, usually, of a simple nature. Curved lamination producing floating forms is a strong interest at the moment. A high level of safety is maintained.

P-14, 2014, mahogany, mahogany and birch veneer, 42" x 22" x 21".
Photo by Schopplein.com

Brandon Skupski

Asheville, North Carolina

Furniture defines a space. It not only dictates the function of a space, but also creates or enhances its style, mood, and character.

I want my work to function in the purest sense. It must be physically comfortable for its use in a setting, while also being aesthetically appropriate. My goal in design is to strip the furniture down to pure form, while maintaining interest in subtleties. I take great pride in my craftsmanship, and add many of the minor nuances of detail that only a handmade object can possess.

Ashlar Chair, 2014, walnut, 28" h x 18" w x 22" d. *Photo by Brandon Skupski*

Pinnate Coffee Table, 2014, walnut, 17" h x 22" w x 42" d. *Photo by Brandon Skupski*

Rouge Chair, 2013, maple, 32" h x 18" w x 22" d. *Photo by Brandon Skupski*

Joshua Smith
Fort Bragg, California

Joshua Smith endeavors to make pieces that utilize and highlight the stories inherent in the wood he uses. He looks for character marks, grain changes, and colors that will support the form he envisions. Often these inform the final piece more than the initial concept sketches.

Low-Back Rocker, 2014, California walnut, Danish cord, teak oil, 33" x 26" x 32". *Photo by David Welter*

Icarus Dress, madrone, Mexican cedar, maple, 48" x 26" x 34". 2014 Faculty Selects Winner, *Exhibited at FS14, the Port Townsend Chapel.*

Freeland Southard
Kokomo, Indiana

Freeland Southard is an Ohio-born artist currently living in Kokomo, Indiana. His work as a general contractor has given him knowledge of construction, materials and collaboration as inspiration for his furniture practice. He loves helping to raise his two boys, and, of course, working in his studio. Freeland received his BFA in ceramics at the Cleveland Institute of Art and his MFA in furniture design from the Herron School of Art and Design.

I enjoy working with materials. Their personalities and attributes provide the chance of a challenge with each intersection. I liken my effort to that of an orchestrator or coordinator, working with the potential of the materials and helping to build the conversation between them. Much as I do with people, I enjoy seeing materials going beyond the convention of prescribed boundaries and expectations. I balance the work by revealing the natural and manicured qualities of the materials. Transparency in the arrangement of these materials is the basis for the narration in the work. I do this in furniture, as it makes sense to make work inspired by people for people to incorporate and use in their environment.

This work is inspired by people and groups that work together with good communication and a cooperative spirit. I believe that is the place where potential is revealed and innovation is found. Also, I like root beer.

Divided Self, 2014, mahogany, cast bronze, mirror, 72" x 54" x 52". *Photo by Dan Fox/Lumina Studio*

Grey Cabinet, 2014, ash, aluminum finish, reclaimed Indiana limestone, stainless steel, brass, glass, 52" x 28" x 16". *Photo by Dan Fox/Lumina Studio*

Jerry Spady
Oak Ridge, Tennessee

I've been seriously interested in woodworking since the early 1970s (actually, I can claim over fifty years' experience, thanks to a few grade-school pieces that my mother kept). However, I come to the field from a life spent in basic research in the biological sciences. Over the years, I have accumulated degrees in zoology, chemistry, and mathematics, and a doctorate in biochemistry, so my woodworking interests are, not surprisingly, experimental in nature.

In 2001, I invented an epoxy/veneer composite material bonded under vacuum. It has proven to be extraordinarily versatile. Since I discovered Fineply, I have explored the material to see what kind of non-traditional forms might be made from it. I'm still following that pathway, and the end is not in sight.

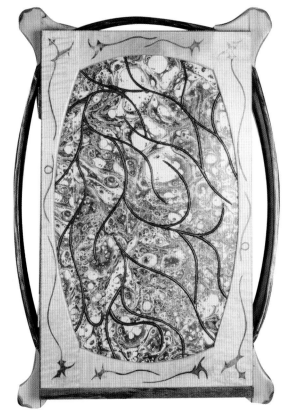

Air Quarium, 68" h x 32" w x 15" d. *Photo by John Lucas*

"Revolution" Cabinet,
wood, 30" x 20" x 8".

a professional title— designer/craftsman?

ALED LEWIS

What do I call myself? You'd think after thirty years of working with wood, making furniture, I'd know. I understand the importance of a professional title. It suggests how I spend my time, and it summarizes, more or less, the approach I take to my work. But am I a studio furniture maker, cabinetmaker, or sculptural artist? I've made and continue to make so many different kinds of furniture that it's difficult to pigeonhole my work into any one category. The titles here would not fit on my business card.

These days we turn our hands to almost anything. We might imagine, as furniture makers, that we are carpenters, joiners, cabinetmakers, chair makers, upholsterers, polishers, and so on. At one time, these jobs were defined, separate and noble professions. I've known men who spent their working lives in one of these trades and were masters of their craft. I'm not arguing here for the respect we should have and might have lost for individual trades; that discussion leads elsewhere. I want to examine this—my professional title.

Many furniture makers now use the term designer/maker to describe their profession. It's a relatively new title, having emerged during the craft revival, and has, over the last thirty or forty years, become the label that perhaps best describes the work I, and many woodworkers like me, perform. This is a hybrid, a combination of the designer whose ideas and inspirations are partly informed by his (or her) craft and knowledge of the materials, and the maker, whose methods and skills are guided by the design.

It is an appropriate two-word title. When the balance between design and making is right, the outcome is unquestionably good. It fails when the designer strives for that instantly recognizable piece, deluded by the desire for fame and notoriety. We may not be able to describe it, but we know when design has become self-conscious. Likewise, when the making takes center stage, the result can be an ostentatious use of complicated form and joinery that ruins the design. Whether it has hand cut dovetails or not is less important than whether it needs dovetails at all. It becomes about the maker not the product, as if he knows the words but does not speak the language of furniture making. So this two-word title wants balance.

Of course, professionals will perceive the weight of these two words in different ways. To some, design may mean self-expression. It might indulge personal notions, political, social, or aesthetic notions that tilt the work heavily toward art furniture, or less functional furniture. For others, self-expression is confined to their knowledge, skills, and design influences, preferring to leave personal beliefs to one side. David Colewell, a talented and respected designer and champion of sustainable methods of furniture manufacturing, expressed an opinion on art furniture by remarking that "to be accepted as art furniture it must first be unaffordable, unusable, and if it is un-makable as well, that clinches it." Whatever opinion is expressed, whether a buyer's obsession with art/sculptural pieces or the craftsman's overindulgence in the "dovetail olympics," we should judge work by the quality of design, its originality and innovation, alongside the flawless making.

I am not solely a designer. I could not cope with being detached from the making process, the hands-on involvement. Neither am I solely a maker, though this is where my career and many others started. I need to be closely involved in the process of conveying the idea to reality, to have the conversation with the client and interpret an aspiration to something that hopefully exceeds expectation. Indeed, the independence that comes with being a designer/maker can be liberating, though in most cases, only if there is a willing, paying client. We would all like to be free to say, "No, that's not what I want to make because it doesn't interest me." Sadly, that is not always possible.

When given the opportunity, I strive to make furniture that resolves a design brief elegantly and skillfully and answers a functional requirement with an aesthetically pleasing solution. For each piece, the technical resolutions are appropriate and sound. I resist the urge to show off my skills unnecessarily and I employ up-to-date technologies where appropriate. I make a living this way, producing what I hope are special, useful, and, sometimes, beautiful pieces for my clients. I fulfill my own criteria for calling myself a designer/maker. My business card wouldn't lie.

Dolly Spragins
Berkeley, California

I am "awakened" to the beauty, diversity, and availability of furniture-grade lumber in urban environments that is mostly lost or mulched. I have used a lot of ash, which is being decimated by the Emerald Ash Borer, in my furniture. It can be creamy white and taupe, simple or extremely sensuous, as in burl veneer, allowing for large visual contrast within a muted palette.

Scavenged volunteer twigs inspire me to explore ways to make something interesting and useful of throw-away material.

Twig Table, twigs and plywood, 18" x 18" x 20". *Exhibited at FS14, the Port Townsend Chapel*

Lady's Desk, reclaimed ash, ash burl, 32" x 37.5" x 30". *Exhibited at FS14, the Port Townsend Chapel.*

Robert Sukrachand

Ridgewood, New York

Robert Sukrachand designs and builds custom furniture in
Brooklyn, New York.

Wishbone Display, 2013, solid walnut,
86" l x 18" d x 40" h. Designed for a
jewelry store in the shape of one of its
signature designs; has ring slots for
displaying jewelry.

Abraham Tesser
Athens, Georgia

Over the years I have developed a set of preferences that almost always find their way into my furniture. Much of my work revolves around showing beautiful wood to advantage. The craft is always there, I hope, but the wood takes the starring role. It is the beauty in wood surfaces that invites me to incorporate unusual and exotic veneers into my work. The default in many wood objects is straight lines and right angles. But wood can also be bent or sculpted into smooth, sensuous curves. I love such nonlinear shapes and they are integral to much of my furniture.

I appreciate the intensely personal aspects of design and construction that come with working alone. Each piece is, for a time, my baby and it is difficult for me to let it go. However, nothing pleases me more than learning that others appreciate the effect that my work has on them; that they like it enough to have it in their home or office.

Rachel's Cabinet, 2013, Japanese tamo ash veneer, walnut veneer, Baltic birch plywood, solid walnut, with black lacquer, wipe-on poly oil over shellac, wax, 41.25" x 44" (closed) or 50" (open) x 18.5". *Photos by Abraham Tesser*

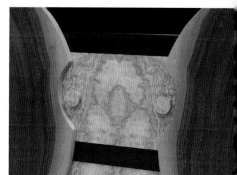

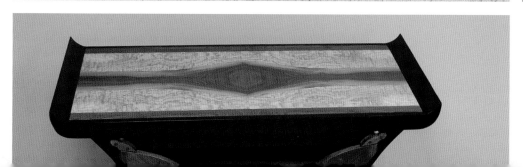

Colin Tury
Sterling Heights, Michigan

To me, craft is important to our culture because it provides us a reminder that we are all still human and that we make things for a reason, not just to look at. Furniture, specifically, shares importance in that we are all unconsciously intimate with it throughout our day. We have lost all sense of material in a sea of powder-coated aluminum and veneered particleboard. I want to present material in furniture for its true nature, and highlight human error because it is a reminder that someone consciously created it. I strive to create conceptual meaning in all my pieces so that it can tell a story beyond its own physical existence. Materials play a big role in this because they have unique, specific, physical attributes that we can obey or abstract. A story can exist just in bringing two materials together in an interesting way.

Transriddance, 2013, white oak, ash, 26" x 47" x 40".
Photo by Colin Tury

Rather a Moment, 2014, maple, steel, 30" x 75" x 38".
Photo by Colin Tury

Despite Our Perceptions, 2013, ash, steel, 22" x 26" x 36".
Photo by Colin Tury

Nicholas Van Gorp

I am a designer and maker rooted in tradition and challenging the contemporary view of furniture to create objects that once again have soul. My intentions are to create new dialogue at the intersection of tradition and innovation.

I make furniture to investigate the connection between soul and craft—the life-long journey of a craftsperson's identity formation. As well, my work is an exploration into the relationship between traditional materials/methods, and contemporary practices to change how we talk about furniture and its history.

Chair, wire, steel, plywood, 39" x 15" x 18". 2014 Faculty Selects Winner, *Exhibited at FS14, the Port Townsend Chapel.*

Paul Wanrooij
Harpswell, Maine

In my work I attempt to capture harmony, beauty, and functionality while creating a piece that is pleasant to the eye—with lines emphasizing unboundedness.

Creating, constructing, and building have always been very fulfilling to me. I built my first pieces in my early twenties. They were simple and basic cabinets, though my friends liked them and were eager to have them in their homes. Later on, I built a fourteen-foot sailboat from some simple drawings. I have to say that I had more fun building the boat than sailing it!

Woodworking is in my genes. I was born and raised in the Netherlands, where my father and uncle were both craftsmen. I feel that through them, I inherited a sense for beauty, harmony, and balance.

After a period of time spent in the managerial world, a career change led to the Fine Woodworking Program at Haywood Community College in North Carolina.

In 2002, I started creating furniture in a small, one-car garage. Since that time, many, many unique pieces of furniture have been created for customers all around the country and beyond.

Oceana Demi-lune, 2007, walnut, maple, 32" h x 42" w x 21" d. *Photo by Paul Wanrooij*

Mark Wedekind
Anchorage, Alaska

As a woodworker and furniture designer/builder, I often work with curved, sculpted shapes and asymmetrical proportions. The inspiration for the furniture I build comes from shapes and patterns that I see in nature: a piece of driftwood, roots wrapping around a rock, the way a branch comes off a gnarly tree trunk. I find these natural lines more appealing and timeless than straight, square, and predictable. Wood is a dynamic and changeable material with which to work. By using time-tested joinery and construction methods that have been used in fine furniture for generations, I can ensure that my pieces will hold together into the next century. Wood is also very sculptable and, as long as I play by its rules, I can challenge both myself and the material to create successful new designs.

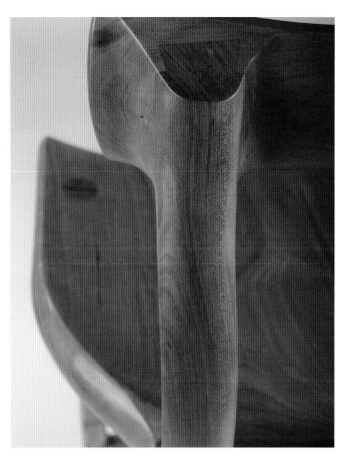

Sculpted Bar Stools, 2013, cherry, river rocks, walnut accents, 42" (to top of seat back)/30" (seat height) x 17.25" w x 18.25" d. *Photos by Anne Raup*

Tom Wessells
Newport News, Virginia

I have included two pieces that are representative of my current work. I have been making a series of small wall cabinets I call "Curiosities." They are a contemporary take on an old furniture tradition. Mine can store curiosities, but I treat the insides in a way that, when one opens them, they are curiosities in and of themselves. The second piece is a bent, laminated arm chair. I have been refining this design for several years. I wanted a chair that worked well and was comfortable and strong, but sleek.

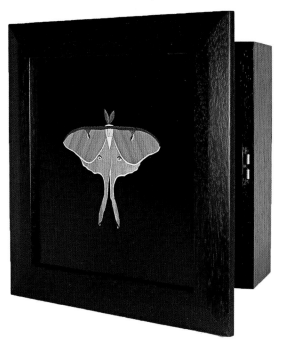

Luna Moth Cabinet, 2012, wenge, dyed and natural veneers, 14" x 14" x 6". *Photo by Tom Wessells*

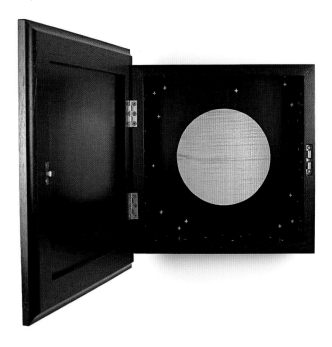

Bent Wood Arm Chair, 2014, walnut (bent/ laminated), cocobolo, leather, 38" x 37" x 24". *Photo by Tom Wessells*

Steve White
Bishop, California

Furniture at its best is equal parts artful design, impeccable craftsmanship, and beautiful material. I strive to create pieces that will be noteworthy for their execution, but will also stand alone as pieces of visual art.

Originally trained as a mechanical engineer, I have for decades drifted art-ward, finding that, although math and structural considerations have great uses in furniture design, numerous art and design classes have given me a great appreciation for aesthetics.

For me, the fascination of this field is the dual disciplines of design and construction, coupled with a lifelong affinity for wood. My designs are contemporary and have evolved into a style that uses the interplay of gentle curves to form unique and elegant compositions. My pieces are built with solid wood and traditional joinery, with the intention that they will increase in value over generations.

Music Stand, 2013, cherry. *Photo by Steve White*

Low Stools, 2014, cherry and maple, 13" or 18" x 14" x 14". *Photo by Steve White*

Mark Whitley

Smiths Grove, Kentucky

Mark Whitley began his journey as a studio furniture maker over 30 years ago. Growing up in a cabinet shop on the family farm in Southern Kentucky, he began to learn traditional methods of furniture making that are the heart of his work today. In a small shop nestled in the outskirts of Smiths Grove, Kentucky, Whitley now creates contemporary, original furniture with sensitivity to materials and unapologetic style.

Blonde River Chest, 2013, maple burl, mahogany, wenge, 18" x 22" x 50". *Photo by Michael Ward Photography*

Music Cabinet, 2013, cherry, ebony, maple, 54" x 20" x 25". *Photo by Michael Ward Photography*

Kevin Wiggers
Beaverton, Ontario, Canada

Born in 1990, Kevin Wiggers's love for using tools and working with wood revealed itself at a very early age. As a young boy, Kevin excelled at sports, especially the game of baseball. He developed a costly habit of breaking bats, and one day asked his father, John, how wooden bats were made. John explained that they were turned on a lathe, similar to the one he had in his shop. This inevitably led to an informal apprenticeship with his grandfather Johan, who taught Kevin how to turn his own wooden bats on the lathe. After graduating from high school, Kevin completed the Woodworking Technician Program at Conestoga College. Since then, Kevin has continued to spend time with his father and grandfather learning additional cabinet-making, veneering, marquetry, inlay, and finishing techniques, including specialized work with unusual natural materials such as parchment, shagreen, and mother-of-pearl. In 2010, Kevin's *Levee Table* was selected by jury for exhibit in the "Faculty Selects" exhibition at The Furniture Society meeting at MIT in Boston. An image of this table was subsequently published in the book *Mind & Hand—Contemporary Studio Furniture*. Now working in a studio space previously shared with his late father, Kevin has taken over all operations of Wiggers Custom Furniture. Additionally, Kevin is in the process of developing a new branch of the business that will showcase the company's long history of craftsmanship on a new range of exquisitely detailed goods targeted at a discerning market.

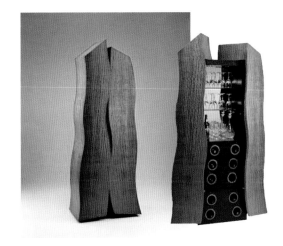

Andiroba Wine Cabinet, 1998, mottled tangare on FSC-certified plywood, glass, mirror, granite, 84" h x 49" w x 25" d. *Photo by John Glos*

Aquaria Desk, 2014, walnut, maple, white deerskin, silk (tassel), sterling silver (escutcheon), 30" x 23" x 47". *Photo by Mandy O'Hara*

Kimberly Winkle
Smithville, Tennessee

Employing traditional furniture making techniques and materials, I build forms and structures with results that are, oftentimes, untraditional. My interest lies in the pursuit and potential of the medium as an expressive device. I use hardwood, paint, and graphite to create my works. The forms are generally streamlined in order to better play the role of an empty canvas for color and line. I activate the wood by painting and drawing onto its surface. This painting is not an act of irreverence for the material; instead I am interested in realizing its potential as something other than its naked self. My color palette is rich yet flat. I animate the painted surface with drawn marks consisting of varied arrangements of lines and dots; the combination of these marks result in an exciting, and somewhat quirky, dialogue of characters. These inscriptions serve as pattern, embellishment, and residual evidence of my hand. I strive to create an apparent sense of spontaneity, chaos with order, rhythm, and gesture with these marks, all working in concert to imbue the object with individuality and charm.

Blanket Chest, 2013, cherry, cedar, MDF, milk paint, brass, 20" h x 58" l x 18" d. *Photo by Tenn. Tech. Univ. Photographic Services*

The Pair: South Union (coat hangers), 2011, cherry, poplar, steel and milk paint, individually: 10" h x 18" l x 6" d. *Photo by Tenn. Tech. Univ. Photographic Services*

Near/Afar Table, 2013, cherry, poplar and milk paint, 36" h x 58" l x 14" d. *Photo by Tenn. Tech. Univ. Photographic Services*

Erik Wolken
Chapel Hill, North Carolina

I have been experimenting with the human figure in my work since the early 2000s. Previous works incorporated totems and masks, and then more biomorphic and gestural forms. My current work approaches the figure in both two- and three-dimensional frameworks. Using abstracted forms of the human figure, I have created a series of small cabinets and tables that are embellished with two-dimensional images of the human form. The two-dimensional images also serve the function of a narrative or documentary element.

The elements of my work, combined with the functional nature of the objects I build, seek to create a powerful dialog between the user and the object, which is at the heart of my artistic goals.

You and Me a Pair of Chairs, 2013, painted poplar and cherry, 37" x 25" x 25". *Photo by Jason Dowdle*

Stewart Wurtz

Seattle, Washington

Stewart Wurtz maintains his studio in the Fremont neighborhood of Seattle. His work is inspired by the minimalism of modern form and design. He embellishes simple forms with small details to reveal process, structure, and the hand of the maker. He uses wood along with other materials, like metal, as the play and dialog between can enhance and complement in unexpected ways.

When I begin a project, my time sketching is indispensable in working through ideas. Often I am inspired by a particular gesture or form in an early sketch that starts the dance of a new piece. The challenge is to keep the freshness of this gesture while continuing to develop the idea. I find myself going back and forth between the drawing and 3-D mock-up until I really understand the essence of this new object. The details and the structure develop out of this exploration and begin to crystallize as I start work on the final piece.

All I can hope for in making my furniture is to pay homage in some small way to the wonder and beauty of our natural environment. I strive for an economy of form in my work and like to use simple lines with spare detail to achieve this balance. My work is meant to be utilitarian, and I'd be honored to think that it will be enjoyed both today and well into the future.

Stools. *Exhibited at FS14, the Port Townsend Chapel.*

Luna Rocker, ebonized walnut, walnut burl, blackened steel, fabric. 24" x 32.5" x 36". *Exhibited in association with FS14 at the Northwest Woodworkers Gallery, Seattle.*

Nico Yektai

Sag Harbor, New York

Nico Yektai is a nationally exhibiting artist who makes one-of-a-kind pieces of functional furniture from his studio outside Sag Harbor. Each component within these pieces of furniture has its own identity. During construction, these components will often push away from their neighbors in a way that calls attention to themselves. The composition is then evaluated by the artist, and other pieces are shifted or faceted to achieve balance. The energy that this sort of construction captures helps make these functional pieces of furniture seductive from afar and more engaging the closer you get. Commission work is an integral part of Yektai's involvement with furniture.

Wall Hung Console #1, 2013, walnut, 12" h x 78" w x 17" d. *Photo by Nico Yektai*

Waves, 2014, bleached maple and cast concrete, 19" h x 94" w x 14" d. *Photo by Nico Yektai*

Tak Yoshino
Yamanashi-ken, Japan

As a furniture maker, the most significant thing I do is to give the maximum respect for the life of the trees I use, making concessions to the wood as the beauty of the wood reveals itself. Traditional Japanese design is congruent with nature, expressing the inherent beauty in everyday design.

The most important aspect of my chairs is based on the practice of Zazen sitting. Zazen is the experience of the harmony of body and soul that we seek to achieve in our daily life. It is a method of sitting where your head and pelvis are in perfect alignment, reducing the stress you encounter throughout the day.

I have developed a method of making personalized chairs which entails fitting the chair to the contours of the pelvis and spine, thus promoting correct posture through Zazen positioning.

Both my Chaise Longue and Zen chairs are an elegant unification of modern day ergonomics, engineering, design and traditional Japanese woodworking, craftsmanship and Zen practices.

Takahiro Yoshino was born in Tokyo in 1958. In 1980, he learned the basics of woodworking from the Shinagawa Training School for Various Professions, studying under Jiro Hayashi, Western furniture maker, and Kenji Suda, Japanese traditional woodcraft artist. In 1986 Tak established the COM Furniture Design Studio in Kawaguchiko, Japan.

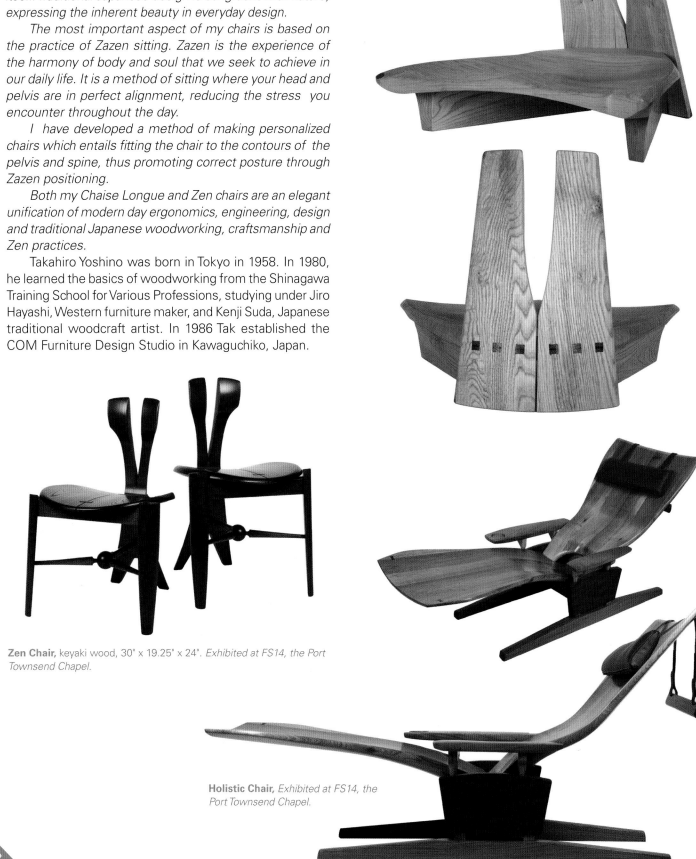

"Mantra" Zen Meditation Chair. *Exhibited at FS14, the Port Townsend Chapel.*

Zen Chair, keyaki wood, 30" x 19.25" x 24". *Exhibited at FS14, the Port Townsend Chapel.*

Holistic Chair, *Exhibited at FS14, the Port Townsend Chapel.*

Moyu Zhang
Rochester, New York

Born and raised in China, educated and practiced in Finland and the United States, Moyu Zhang was an architect when she realized she wanted to actually make the things she was designing. She set aside her architecture degree and eight years of work experience, and enrolled in RIT's furniture design MFA program. Much of her work is a mixture of sculptural and functional, and shows her interest in the materiality of wood. She currently is in her thesis year in the School for American Crafts.

Seating for Two, 2012, ash, zebra wood, purple heart, wenge, padauk, 21.5" h x 37" w x 31.5" d. *Photo by Moyu Zhang*

Black Ribbon, 2012, ash, 15.5" h x 24" w x 25.25" d. *Photo by Moyu Zhang*

Jeremy Zietz
Shrewsbury, Vermont

The chest's inspiration is from early American folk pieces that were often elaborately decorated, typically painted. Johannes Spitler and other German-Americans popularized this idea. The "tree of life" spins upward from its seed, which roots itself below. The tree is a ubiquitous symbol of growth that connects all forms of life.

Tree of Life Chest, 2013, black walnut, maple inlay, 35" w x 20.5" d x 48.374" t. *Photos by Jeremy Zietz*

reforestation: how to make a tree from a chair

ANNE BRENNAN & ASHLEY JAMESON ERIKSMOEN

I am standing in an unlikely grove. The branches of one tree are raised stiffly skywards, sprouting rigid, spear-shaped leaves at regular intervals. The elaborate ridged bole of another tapers upwards to terminate in a crown of heavily stiff and formal-looking foliage. Yet another looks like a spindly, unstable tower of untamed growth, its branches sprouting from unexpected places, as though it has been badly pruned or attempting to regenerate after a bushfire.

The most remarkable yet obvious thing about these trees is that they are assembled from dismantled pieces of furniture, and no attempt has been made to hide this fact. The branches, leaves, and trunks plainly bear the evidence of their previous lives as spindles from a bedstead, the arm or seat of a chair, or the turned base of a dining room table. Even the limed paint and cheap varnish with which they were originally dressed has been left intact.

This little grove is the fruit of Ashley Eriksmoen's recent obsession with the Green Shed in Mugga Lane, where Canberra's unwanted items go to be recycled. Her focus has been on the most abject items in an already abject collection: the furniture that has been discarded because it is broken and is therefore unsellable even in a secondhand market. The damage to these items is often slight—nothing that couldn't be repaired with a screw or a dab of glue. However, they have been designed to hold together just long enough to reach the limit of their fashionableness, so no one has bothered to fix them, because why repair something that will no longer fit in with a new décor?

One hundred fifty years ago, the value of a piece of furniture was invested in its utility, so that its life might span several human generations, or eighty to a hundred years. This would be long enough for the tree that replaced the one from which the item was made to grow to full maturity. These days, the life of a piece of furniture may be as little as ten to fifteen years, not nearly enough time for the regeneration of the trees that have been sacrificed for it.

This waste is multiplied further when you consider the size of the manufacturing enterprises that feed our appetite for novelty and change. So, at a time when global warming preoccupies us, and the watchword for designers is sustainability, Ashley Eriksmoen proposes a question that brings these issues to the forefront of our consciousness: rather than harvesting trees to make furniture, what would happen if we were to harvest furniture to make trees?

Ecru Cabriole Tree: 2620 x 1120 x 1000mm (tree); Four ecru dining chairs with Cabriole legs. **Chair #39:** 830 x 430 x 430mm (chair) *Photo by Art Atelier Photography*

In this project, the processes of a furniture maker and a gardener become analogous. Ashley assembles and archives her repertoire of furniture fragments with all the care of a fine cabinetmaker gathering and itemizing a collection of rare timbers. At the same time, these fragments stacked in an orderly fashion against the wall of her workspace, remind me of a collection of rootstock in a nursery. Each tree requires complex joinery techniques to unite the constituent parts into a new whole. But in her careful cutting, splicing, and joining, it is also possible to read an analogy with grafting, the nurseryman's painstaking union of rootstock and introduced plant or scion.

The purpose of grafting is to introduce new genetic material to the host plant for some kind of advantage, to create a more vigorous and fruitful plant, for example, or to hasten the production of a hybrid, combining desirable aesthetic properties, or to reproduce plants that cannot easily be propagated by other means.

Grafting is also used to create curiosities—a sort of virtuoso exhibition of the nurseryman's art, in which a plant can be made to bear both potatoes and tomatoes, or several different plants can be spliced together in complex ways to create a trellised effect. Such exhibitions of skill always seem to have, at their heart, a desire for human mastery of the unpredictable and organic ways of the botanical world.

There is something of this at play in Ashley's trees, underscored by the ways in which craft privileges skill for its own sake and ascribes to craftsmanship a particular form of aesthetic pleasure. But for all the skill and labor Ashley has lavished upon bringing these objects into being, they remain awkward and ungainly, more remarkable for the unlikeliness of their state than for any inherent beauty they may possess. Ultimately, then, the intensively laboured nature of Ashley's project exists solely to gesture toward the intrinsic impossibility of its fundamental proposition.

—Anne Brennan

Ashley Jameson Eriksmoen studied fine woodworking at the College of the Redwoods; MFA in furniture design at Rhode Island School of Design. Eriksmoen is a furniture designer/maker who exhibits internationally. She has taught at California College of the Arts, College of the Redwoods, Oregon College of Art & Craft, Anderson Ranch Arts Center, Penland School of Craft and, is currently the head of furniture at Australian National University (ANU) School of Art.

Anne Brennan is a writer and artist; she is the head of the Art Theory Workshop of the ANU School of Art.

Mission Brown Bud Tree with **Chair #30:** 2600 x 1800 x 1670mm (tree) and 840 x 425 x 425mm (chair); four large diameter turned bedposts, four square sectioned dining table legs, curved back rail of dining chair, spindled head and footboards from twin bed, one crib rail, blanket stand with turned legs. *Photo by Art Atelier Photography*

Oval Leaf Tree with **Chair #11:** 2550 x 1250 x 1250mm (tree) and 990 x 480 x 430 (chair); Spindled head and footboards of twin bunk bed, blanket stand with turned legs, turned legs from dining chair, single round leg. *Photo by Art Atelier Photography*

Blonde Palm Tree with **Chair #33:** 2125 x 2300 x 2300mm (tree) and 830 x 470 x 470mm (chair); Four large diameter turned table legs, twin bed spindled head and footboards, turned pedestal table base, four slat backed dining chairs. *Photo by Art Atelier Photography*

contacts

MEMBERS

Robert Aibel
Moderne Gallery
111 N. 3rd St.
Philadelphia, PA 19106
Email: raibel@aol.com
Web: www.modernegallery.com

Robert Aiosa
Madison, WI 53704
Email: aiosarobert@gmail.com

Joshua Almond
Rollins College
1000 Holt Ave. – 2774
Winter Park, FL 32789
Email: ralston_piper@hotmail.com
Web: www.joshalmond.com

Jerry Alonzo
Email: jerry.alonzo@gmail.com

Farida Alrashaid
22 Kinross Rd.
Greylees, Sleaford NG 34 8 GF
United Kingdom
Email: rushfrida@gmail.com
Web: www.theheartofart.com

Judith Ames
2118 East Olive St.
Seattle, WA 98122
Email: jgholzerames@aol.com

Jonathan Amson
11000 Kings Crown Drive
Prospect, KY 40059
Email: jonathan.amson@verizon.net

Brian Anderson
Email: a.woodworks@hotmail.com

Samantha Anderson
Email: sanderso@risd.edu

Hayami Arakawa
85 EliotAve.
West Newton, MA 02465
Email: hayami@mit.edu

Flat Rate Exchange: Art/Design Team
111 Sheridan St. Apt 2
portland, ME 04101
Email: flatrateexchange@gmail.com
Web: www.flatrateexchange.wordpress.com/design-
     exchange/

Heather Ashworth
440 Utterback Rd.
Murray, KY 42071
Email: heather4trees@yahoo.com

Wally Auclair
73 Maple Leaf Road Box 36
Glendale, RI 02820
Email: wafurniture@hotmail.com

Teresa Audet
2420 Blaisdell Ave. S
Minneapolis, MN 55404
Email: TeresaAudet@gmail.com
Web: www.TeresaAudet.com

Terry Bachman
Tangram Woodworks
424 Virginia Ave.
Cumberland, MD 21502
Email: terry@tangramwoodworks.com
Web: www.tangramwoodworks.com

Russell Baldon
943 42nd St.
Oakland, CA 94608
Email: russellbaldon@gmail.com
Web: www.russell-baldon.squarespace.com

Marc Balentine
19261 Basin View Dr.
Fort Bragg, CA 95437
Email: marcbalentine@gmail.com

Martha Barbour
3333B Industrial Dr.
Durham, NC 27704
Email: martha@shopbottools.com

John Barfield
2833 Pembroke Rd.
Toledo, OH 43606
Email: barfielddesign@gmail.com
Web: www.johnbarfielddesign.com

Beston Barnett
3020 Dale St.
San Diego, CA 92104
Email: beston@cox.net
Web: www.bestonbarnett.com

Carl Bass
Autodesk
47 OakvaleAve.
Berkeley, CA 94705
Email: carl.bass@autodesk.com

Angelo Battisti
35 Pondview Dr.
Allentown, NJ 08501-1602
Email: angelmarkjames@usa.net

Bennett Bean
Bennett Bean Studio
357 Main St.
Blairstown, NJ 07825
Email: bennettbean@bennettbean.com

Jim Becker
Jas. Becker Cabinetmaker, LLC
254 Barnumville Rd. Manchester Center, VT 05255
P.O. Box 802
Wilder, VT 05088
Email: james@jasbecker.com
Web: www.jasbecker.com

Susan Beckerman
685 West End Ave. Apt 9c
New York, NY 10025
Email: sb1118@aol.com

Lars Beeghley
LBB Woodworking
28527 Amborella Way
Menifee, CA 92584
Email: lbb4506@msn.com

Vivian Beer
21 Dow St.
Manchester, NH 03101
Web: www.vivianbeer.com

Joseph Bennett
112 N 13th St Apt 4
Murray, KY 42071
Email: Jbennett26@murraystate.edu

Kayla Bennett
44 N Main St.
Stewartstown, PA 17363
Email: kb2938@gmail.com

Nils Berg
Email: info@nilsbergfurniture.com

Allison Bigbee
101 West Croydon Court
Easley, SC 29642
Email: abigbeedesign@yahoo.com

Marc Bilbao
630 Winklers Creek
Boone, NC 28607
Email: bilbaomj@appstate.edu

Jonathan Binzen
14 Pleasant St.
New Milford, CT 06776
Email: jbinzen@snet.net

Virginia Birchfield
Email: gin@virginiabirchfieldinteriors.com

Thomas Birkeness
8 OakAve.
Colorado Springs, CO 80906
Email: mastercraftsman@birkeness.com

Mark Bixby
7204 NE Bake Hill Rd.
Bainbridge Island, WA 98110
Email: tfs@markbixby.com

Ted Blachly
PO Box 216
Warner, NH 03278
Email: tedblachly@gmail.com
Web: www.tedblachly.com

Kim Black
1339 Downing St.
Denver, CO 80218
Email: kcblackk@msn.com

Juan Pablo Blanco
Calle 138 # 75-75
Torre 1 Apto 402
Bogota, Cundinamarca
Colombia
Email: juanpix@gmail.com

Eben Blaney
Eben Blaney Fine Contemporary Furniture
96 Eddy Rd.
Edgecomb, ME 04555
Email: eben@ebenblaney.com
Web: www.ebenblaney.com

Ahron Block
Email: blockwood92@gmail.com

Roslyn Bock
Maloof Foundation
PO Box 8051
Alta Loma, CA 91701
Email: maloof@earthlink.net

David Bohnhoff
Bohnhoff Woodworking
3925 Fourcee Farms Lane
Columbia, VA 23038
Email: bohnhoffwoodworking@gmail.com
Web: www.bohnhoffwoodwork.com

Anne Bossert
1624 S. Whitcomb St.
Fort Collins, CO 80526
Email: annebossert@yahoo.com
Web: www.AnneBossertArt.com

James Bowie
Email: jimmybowie@gmail.com

Chris Bowman
1451 W. Stop 11 Rd.
Indianapolis, IN 46217
Email: spoke75@hotmail.com
Web: www.chrisbowmanstudio.com

Shannon Bowser
223 22nd St. Apt 3
Brooklyn, NY 11232
Email: shannon@bowser.org

Don Braden
Email: dbraden0101@yahoo.com

Bruce Bradford
Bradford Custom Furniture
763 Barnsdale Rd.
Winston Salem, NC 27106
Email: maker@bradfordcustomfurniture.com
Web: www.bradfordcustomfurniture.com/

Todd Bradlee
TB Furniture
336 Hammond St.
Bishop, CA 93514
Email: toddbradlee@gmail.com

Robert Bragg
36349 Lee Highway
Glade Spring, VA 24340
Email: rbraggdesigns@aol.com

Timothy Brauer
University of Colorado, Denver
Campus Box 126
P.O. Box 173364
Denver, CO 80217
Email: timothy.j.brauer@ucdenver.edu

Scott Braun
4811 Vernon Blvd. # 2
Long Island City, NY 11101
Email: scottbraunfurniture@gmail.com

Cindy Braunheim
Email: braunheim@msn.com

Xander Bremer
Email: xander@xanderbremer.com

Michael Brolly
1405 ChelseaAve.
Bethlehem, PA 18018
Email: brollywood@aol.com

Garrett Brooks
42 Division Ave. S
Grand Rapids, MI 49503
Email: gnevillebrooks@gmail.com

Robert Brou
Naturalism Furniture
1564 DeKalb Ave. #5
Atlanta, GA 30307
Email: info@naturalismfurniture.com
Web: www.naturalismfurniture.com

Greg Brown
63 Nottingham Rd.
Deerfield, NH 03037
Email: gbwoodworks@hotmail.com
Web: www.gbwoodworks.com

Michael Brown
Michael Brown Chairmaker
56 Cedar Gut Lane
Grantsboro, NC 28529
Email: michael@michaelbrownchairmaker.com
Web: www.michaelbrownchairmaker.com

Rob Brown
Equinox Interiors
928 Sherbrooke St.
Peterborough, ON K9J 2R5
Canada
Email: rob@equinoxinteriors.ca
Web: www.equinoxinteriors.ca

Tom Brown
2547 8th #27
Berkeley, CA 94710
Email: brownsack@mac.com

Andy Buck
Rochester Institute of Technology
1629 W. Bloomfield Rd.
Honeoye Falls, NY 14472
Email: aabsac@rit.edu

Stoel Burrowes
1108 E. Franklin St.
Chapel Hill, NC 27415
Email: s_burrow@uncg.edu

Todd Butler
3851 NE Campus Lane
Bremerton, WA 98311
Email: info@thebutlerdidit.ws

Bob Butow
1701 Chain Dam Rd.
Easton, PA 18045
Email: chaindam@yahoo.com

David Calvin
David Calvin Furniture Studio
2222 16th Ave. N
St. Petersburg, FL 33713
Email: dcfurniturestudio@att.net
Web: www.dcfurniturestudio.com

Graham Campbell
1560 Craft Center Dr.
Smithville, TN 37166
Email: gcampbell@tntech.edu
Web: www.tntech.edu/craftcenter

Phil Campbell
1030 W. 38th St.
Baltimore, MD 21211
Email: pcampbell358@cavtel.net

Jeffrey Campeau
Evergreen State College
417 18th Ave. SE
Olympia, WA 98501
Email: skcm_jc@yahoo.com

Arlene Caplan
23 Loantaka Lane North
Morristown, NJ 07928
Email: accrafts@aol.com

Jeff Carter
14 B Gilbert St.
West Haven, CT 06516
Email: jeff@westmountgroup.com
Web: www.westmountgroup.com/

Bill Castonia
706 N. James St.
Ludington, Michigan 49431
Email: billcastonia@aol.com

Kristopher Chan
4013 S. Burns St.
Seattle, WA 98118
Email: krisc16@uw.edu

Colin Chase
Email: chasesculpture@gmail.com

Peter Chen
Email: casikamodern@yahoo.com

Vivian Chiu
925 Fulton Street, Apt #3
Brooklyn, NY 11238
Email: vchiu@risd.edu
Web: www.vivianchiudesigns.com

Leslie Cislo
1847 16th St.
Wyandotte, MI 48192
Email: lessfunctional@yahoo.com

Brandy Clements & Dave Klingler
Silver River Center for Chair Caning
9 Riverside Dr.
Asheville, NC 28806
Email: SilverRiverChairs@gmail.com
Web: www.SilverRiverChairs.com

Bill Clinton
School of Architecture
216 Lindley Pl.
Bozeman, MT 59717
Email: wclinton@montana.edu

Chance Coalter
Chance Studios
3168 Mt. Tami Dr.
San Diego, CA 92111
Email: chancecoalter@gmail.com
Web: www.chancecoalter.com

Randy Cochran
402 5th St. SW
Fort Payne, AL 35967
Email: randy@woodstudio.com

Jim Coffey
3663 54Ave.
Innisfail, AB T4G 1E7
Canada
Email: coffeyj1@telus.net

Byron Conn
Byron Conn Design, LLC
387 W Squire Dr. APT 6
Rochester, NY 14623
Email: byronconndesign@gmail.com
Web: www.byronconn.com

Martha Connell
158 Rumson Rd.
Atlanta, GA 30305
Email: connellgallery@bellsouth.net

Shawn Connor
3971 Green St.
Harrisburg, PA 17110
Email: shawn@connorartistry.com
Web: www.connorartistry.com

John Conrad
Email: john.conrad@asfd.com

Edward Cooke, Jr.
Yale University/Dept. of the History of Art
26 LowellAve.
Newtonville, MA 02460-1612
Email: edward.cooke@yale.edu

Michael Cooper
11547 Green Valley Rd.
Sebastopol, CA 95472
Email: gaylecooper@comcast.net

Paula Cooperrider
8925 West Longmeadow Dr.
Prescott, AZ 86305
Email: paula@cooperrider.org

Joseph Corigliano
16 Tempe Wick Rd.
Mendham, NJ 07945-1814
Email: corigljj@verizon.net
Web: www.jjcfurnituremaker.com

Timothy Cozzens
332 N. GroveAve.
Oak Park, IL 60302
Email: tcozzens@colum.edu

Rick Crangle
30 Bennett St N
Gloucester, MA 01930
Email: rickcrangle@mac.com
Web: www.richardcrangle.com

Michael Crawshaw
955 Hereward Rd.
Victoria, British Columbia V9A 4E1
Canada
Email: m.crawshaw@shaw.ca

Ruth Cross
250 West Main St.
Charlottesville, VA 22902
Email: RCross1066@aol.com

Richard Culp
1815 Parade Grounds Ave. NE
Bainbridge Island, WA 98110
Email: dndculp@cox.net

Matthew X. Curry
Web: www.matthewxcurry.com

Gary Daab
Email: gary@verdant-designs.com

Michael Danchak
339 Oxbow Rd.
Durham, CT 06422
Email: misha@danchakwoodworks.com

Brooke Davis
8204 N. Lamar Ste. B16
Austin, TX 78705
Email: brookemdavisdesign@gmail.com

Maxwell Davis
4824 Park Rd.
Ann Arbor, MI 48103
Email: maxwelldavis@comcast.net

Ross Day
Ross Day Fine Furniture
22828 Rulling Ave. NE
Poulsbo, WA 98370
Email: rorjrday@embarqmail.com

Brian Days
6 March Rd.
Wilmington, MA 01887
Email: briandays@verizon.net

Michael de Forest
12275 NW Old Quarry Rd.
Portland, OR 97229-4735
Email: deforestmh@comcast.net
Web: www.MichaelDeForestStudio.com/

John DeHoog
Email: jdehoog@emich.edu

Sybil Delgaudio
201 East 19 St.
New York, NY 10003
Email: sybil.delgaudio@hofstra.edu

David Delthony
Sculptured Furniture
PO Box 437, 1540 W. Hwy 12
Escalante, UT 84726-0437
Email: ddelth@scinternet.net
Web: www.SculpturedFurnitureArtandCeramics.com

Robert Denlinger
2938 Avenida Valera
Carlsbad, CA 92009
Email: rhdenlinger@gmail.com

Donald Denmeade
Denmeade Fine Woodworking
7782 Tackabury Rd.
Canastota, NY 13032
Email: don@denmeadefww.com
Web: www.denmeadefww.com

John Dennison
2000 Bazan Bay Rd.
North Saanich, BC V8L 1C5
Canada
Email: jdennison@shaw.ca

Scott DeWaard
4132 Rocky Branch Rd.
Walland, TN 37886
Email: sdewaard@bellsouth.net

Forest Dickey
170 Parnassus Ave #6
San Francisco, CA 94117
Email: forest@variandesigns.com

Alicia Dietz
5911 Shrubbery Hill Rd.
Richmond, VA 23227
Email: alicia.dietz8@gmail.com
Web: www.aliciadietz.com

Jack Dodds
2048 Kaiser Rd.
Galien, MI 49113
Email: Drjdodds@csinet.net

Tom & Jennifer Dolese
Web: www.terrafirmadesignnw.com

Norman Doll
11349 N Linnwood Ln
Mequon, WI 53092
Email: normdoll@gmail.com
Web: www.normdolldesigns.com

Steffanie Dotson
1054 Devonshire Dr.
San Diego, CA 92107
Web: www.steffaniedotson.com

William Doub
William Doub Custom Furniture
PO Box 95
Deerfield, NH 03037
Email: wood@shore.net

Martha Downs
3979 Hwy JJ
Black Earth, WI 53515
Email: info@downsworks.com

Ray Duffey
555 Woodruff Place Middle Dr.
Indianapolis, IN 46201
Email: mrayduffey@gmail.com

Chris Dutch
713 White Oak Rd.
Charleston, WV 25302
Email: chrisdutchstainedglass@gmail.com

William Dyckman
1050 Stannage Ave,
Albany, CA 94706
Email: will@dyckmandesign.com

Chris Dykman
2213 Ayum Rd.
Sooke, BC V9Z 0E7
Canada
Email: chris.dykman@gmail.com

Fred Eiden
4616 New Sweden Rd NE
Bainbridge Island, WA 98110
Email: fredeiden@yahoo.com

Carley Eisenberg
Iron Mountain Forge
156 Hanging Rock Villas, #221
Seven Devils, NC 28604
Email: info@carleyeisenberg.com
Web: www.carleyeisenberg.com

Gregory Elder
Dartmouth College
599 Downer Forest Rd.
Sharon, VT 05065
Email: gregory.elder@dartmouth.edu

Nicholas English
Email: honedesigncollab@gmail.com

Christopher Enright
2592 Rio Bravo Circle
Sacramento, CA 95826
Email: cnuchris@yahoo.com
Web: www.flickr.com/photos/canoechris/sets/

Walt Enterline
Enterline Woodworks
2420 Bluff St.
Boulder, CO 80304
Email: walt.enterline@gmail.com
Web: www.enterlinewoodworks.com

Robert and Tor Erickson
Erickson Woodworking
18977 Wepa Way
Nevada City, CA 95959
Email: info@ericksonwoodworking.com
Web: www.ericksonwoodworking.com

Ashley Eriksmoen
Australian National University
105 Childers St.
School of Art Furniture Workshop
Acton, ACT 2601
Australia
Email: ashley.eriksmoen@anu.edu.au
Web: www.soa.anu.edu.au/furniture

Karen Ernst
301 Dundon Rd.
Edinboro, PA 16412
Email: kernst@edinboro.edu

Jung In Eun
68 Overlea Crescent
Kitchener, Ontario N2M 5A9
Canada
Email: eun.canada@gmail.com

Phill Evans
7958 Entrance St.
Fair Oaks, CA 95628-7106
Email: phillart@sbcglobal.net
Web: www.phillevans.com

Thomas Fetherston
50 De Haro St.
San Francisco, CA 94103
Email: thomas@customfurnituredesign.com

Karl Fiebig
Email: karl.fiebig@yahoo.com

Brian Fireman
Brian Fireman Design
205-B Lexington Rd.
Landrum, SC 29356
Email: brianfireman@hotmail.com
Web: www.brianfiremandesign.com

Fabian Fischer
Email: contact@ffhandcrfts.com

Irving Fischman
106 Summer St.
Somerville, MA 02143
Email: irvingfischman@alum.mit.edu

Darren Fisher
1 Walling Terrace
Keyport, NJ 07735
Email: d_fisher925@yahoo.com

Dennis FitzGerald
12 Tower Hill Rd.
Pawling, NY 12564
Email: fitzgerald.dennis@gmail.com

Michael Fitzpatrick
43 Church St.
Westborough, MA 01581
Email: mfitz@bostonfurnituremaker.com

David Fleming
5302 East Nisbet Rd.
Scottsdale, AZ 85254
Email: david@dfcabinetmaker.com
Web: www.dfcabinetmaker.com

Ian Fleury
2530 AveburyAve.
Victoria, BC V8R 3V9
Canada
Email: theadventuresofgeorgendragon@hotmail.com

J. Michael Floyd
810 W. 9th St.
Cookeville, TN 38501
Email: jmichaelfloyd@aol.com

Reuben Foat
2722-3 Reynard Way #A
San Diego, CA 92103
Email: reubenfoat@yahoo.com

Robert Foedisch
Email: bobandtory@comcast.net

Mats Fogelvik
Fogelvik Furniture
Po Box 377475
Ocean View, HI 96737
Email: mats@fogelvik.com
Web: www.fogelvik.com/

Amy Forsyth
21 Merkle Rd.
Bechtelsville, PA 19505
Email: amf3@lehigh.edu
Web: www.amyforsyth.com/

Helena Foster
Email: hrfoster@comcast.net

Jason Frantz
1303 E Cambridge
Springfield, MO 65804
Email: jfrantz@woodshopartisans.com
Web: www.woodshopartisans.com

Gail Fredell
PO Box 467
Westport Point, MA 02791
Email: gail@gailfredell.com
Web: gailfredell.com

Claire Fruitman
North Bennet Street School
150 North St.
Williamsburg, MA 02109
Email: clairefruitman@gmail.com

Ken Frye
PO Box 14844
San Luis Obispo, CA 93406
Email: ken@kenfrye.com
Web: www.kenfrye.com

Mike Fulop
433 Avenue G South
Saskatoon, SK s7m1v5
Canada
Email: emptyfull@hotmail.com

Robert Galusha
12010 Hwy 290 West
Suite 170
Austin, TX 78737
Email: galushar@aol.com

Paula Garbarino
16 Ivaloo St.
Somerville, MA 02143
Email: pgarbarino@mac.com
Web: www.pgarbarino.com

Jeff Gard
Email: jag@jagmodern.com

Blaise and Cali Gaston
Blaise Gaston Inc.
686 FairhopeAve.
Earlysville, VA 22936
Email: mail@blaisegaston.com
Web: www.blaisegaston.com

Bryan Geary
7241 Willow Way
Dartmouth, PA 16415
Email: brygeary@gmail.com
Web: www.Brygeary.com

Jordan Gehman
Email: jgehman2121@gmail.com

Jonathan Gerspach
1257 S. Huron St.
Denver, CO 80223
Email: Ghwllc@gmail.com

Nick Gibbs
Freshwood Publishing
4711 Hope Valley Rd.
Durham, NC 27707
Email: nick.gibbs@freshwoodpublishing.com

McKenzie Gibson
Email: cgibson@risd.edu

Brian Gladwell
2334 College Ave Apt C
Regina, SK S4P 1C7
Canada
Email: bgladwell@accesscomm.ca

Andrew Glantz
Zenith Design
5450 E. Cortez Dr.
Scottsdale, AZ 85254
Web: www.zenith-design.com

Andrew Glasgow
135 Lookout Dr.
Asheville, NC 28804
Email: arsv164@aol.com

Sophie Glenn
66 Avenue A, Apt. 5F
New York, NY 10009
Email: sophielydaglenn@gmail.com

Michael Gloor
Michael Gloor Design
24A Dorset Mill Rd.
Exeter, RI 02822
Email: mgloor@gloordesign.com
Web: www.gloordesign.com

Kendall Glover
4858 South Evans Ave.
Chicago, IL 60615
Email: kglover@conjurecraft.com

Martin Goebel
Goebel & Co. Furniture
2936 Locust St.
Saint Louis, MO 63103
Email: info@goebelfurniture.com
Web: www.goebelfurniture.com

Miguel Gomez-Ibanez
North Bennet Street School
150 North St.
Boston, MA 02109
Email: gomez-ibanez@msn.com
Web: www.nbss.edu/

Nicholas Goulden
Email: nagoulden477@gmail.com

Duncan Gowdy
45 South Rd.
Holden, MA 01520
Email: duncan@duncangowdy.com
Web: duncangowdy.com

Marc Grainer
10615 Belfast Pl.
Potomac, MD 20854-1760
Email: dmgrainer@comcast.net

Stuart Green
Email: Stuart+green@gmail.com

Scott Grove
Green Grove Design
31 Riverview Dr.
Rochester, NY 14623
Email: scott@scottgrove.com
Web: www.scottgrove.com/

Glen Guarino
Guarino Furniture Designs
549 Pompton Ave.
Suite 125
Cedar Grove, NJ 07009-1720
Email: guarinofurniture@icloud.com
Web: www.guarinofurnituredesigns.com

Charles Gudaitis
Vachead Designs LLC
118 Blackbeard Dr.
Slidell, LA 70461
Email: vachead@gmail.com
Web: www.vachead.com

Ken Guenter
2549 Forbes St.
Victoria, BC V8R 4B9
Canada
Email: kenguenter@shaw.ca

Erik Gustafson
Email: erik@egwoodworking.com

Nathaniel Hall
4305 Corinth St.
San Diego, CA 92115
Email: rxmaderadesign@gmail.com
Web: www.rxmadera.com

Warren G. Hall
ShopBot Tools
3333 Industrial Dr.
Durham, NC 27704
Email: ted@shopbottools.com

Michael Hamilton
122 North Water St.
Port Hadlock, WA 98339
Email: mhamilton@olympus.net
Web: www.michaelhamiltonfurniture.com

Jennifer Hancock
3126 W. Cary St #156
Richmond, VA 23221
Email: bookzen@comcast.net

Tyra Hanson
The Gallery at Somes Sound
1112 Main St.
PO Box 203
Mount Desert, ME 04660
Email: tyra@galleryatsomessound.com
Web: www.galleryatsomessound.com/

Mateo Hao
47 Boardman Place
San Francisco, CA 94103
Email: mateo.hao@gmail.com

Rob Hare
130 Carney Rd.
Ulster Park, NY 12487
Email: info@robhare-furnituremaker.com
Web: www.robhare-furnituremaker.com

Alan Harp
Web: www.alanharpdesign.com

J. Michael Harriagan
Architectural Accents
9760 Indiana Parkway
Munster, IN 46321
Email: Mike@archaccents.com
Web: www.archaccents.com/

BA Harrington
470 S 11th St, 115 Sprowls Hall
Indiana, PA 15705
Email: harri@iup.edu
Web: www.baharrington.com

Jesse Harrington
Harrington Design Studio
3352 Tilden St.
Philadelphia, PA 19129
Email: jesse@harringtondesignstudio.com
Web: www.harringtondesignstudio.com

Bryan Harris
6 McPhee Place
Curtin, ACT 2605
Email: nobuharris@yahoo.com

Peter Harrison
Web: www.peterharrison.com

Jennifer Harvie-Watt
1526 7thAve.
San Francisco, CA 94122
Email: harviewatt@hotmail.com

Doug Haslam
1520 4th St. NW
Calgary, AB T2M 2Y9
Canada
Email: dahaslam@shaw.ca

John Hatlestad
1830 N. Rte. 83
Unit 1
Grayslake, IL 60030
Email: johnghatlestad@gmail.com

Ian Hawes
c/o Yestermorrow
7869 Main St.
Waitsfield, VT 05673
Email: ebobhawes@gmail.com

Kate Hawes
Kate Hawes Inc.
250 44th St. #309
Brooklyn, NY 11232
Email: kvhawes@gmail.com
Web: www.katehawes.net

Austin Heitzman
Email: charlesaustinh@gmail.com

Paul Henry
Paul Henry Furniture
1905 Crest Dr
Encinitas, CA 92024
Email: paul@paulhenryfurniture.com

Jason A. Hernandez
Email: jasonahernandez@hotmail.com

Sabina Hill
Sabina Hill Design Inc.
110 Brew St.
#302
Port Moody, BC V3H 0E4
Canada
Email: sabina@sabinahill.com
Web: www.sabinahill.com

Noah Hillis
61 Issaquah Dock
Sausalito, CA 91316
Email: nhillis@cca.edu

Anat Hodish
3236 Monument Dr.
Ann Arbor, MI 48108
Email: hodishi@hotmail.com

Rolf Hoeg
Email: rolfhoeg@icloud.com

Stephen Hogbin
Web: www.stephenhogbin.com

Alexis Holcombe
4000 Massachusetts Ave., NW
Apt. 1223
District of Columbia, DC 20016
Email: lexy.holcombe@gmail.com

Steven Holdaway
Email: steveholdaway2@gmail.com

John Holden
Cody Furnishings
7757 Prairie Shadow Rd.
San Diego, CA 92126
Email: johnholden@codyfurnishings.com
Web: www.codyfurnishings.com

Donna Holmquist
15305 Hilding Ave. SE
Monroe, WA 98272
Email: dona61228@gmail.com

Hank Holzer & Judith Ames
Holzerames Furniture
2118 East Olive St.
Seattle, WA 98122
Email: hank@holzerames.com

Ellie Horsnell
916 27thAve.
seattle, DE 98122
Email: elliehorsnell@gmail.com

Richard Hubbs
Email: Rkhubbs@yahoo.com

Katie Hudnall
2340 N. Delaware St.
Indianapolis, IN 46205
Email: katiehudnall@hotmail.com
Web: www.katiehudnall.com

Shane Hughes
18823 Six Mile Rd.
Huson, MT 59846
Email: hugheswoodworks@hotmail.com

Dan Hunt
Email: dthunt@att.net

Robert Huskey
4209 9th Ave NW
Seattle, WA 98107
Email: Bob@saturndesign.com

Matt Hutton
Studio 24b
24 Mayfield St.
Portland, ME 04103
Email: mhutton@meca.edu
Web: www.studio24b.com

Stephen Hynson
Stephen Hynson Fine Furniture
88 Nohea Place
Haiku, HI 96708
Email: stephenhynson@europa.com
Web: www.stephenhynson.com

Michael Iannone
8 Deptford Rd., Unit B
Glassboro, NJ 08028
Email: mi@iannonedesign.com
Web: www.iannonedesign.com

Brenden James
Box 11
Big Lake, BC V0L 1G0
Canada
Email: brendenjames@ymail.com

Brad Jirka
2591 89th Ct. W.
Northfield, MN 55057
Email: brad@bohemiawerks.com

C Larry Johnson
PO Box 186
Waitsburg, WA 99361
Email: claudelarry@hotmail.com

Carl Johnson
1609 N. Franklin St.
Tampa, FL 33602
Email: carljohnson@tampabay.rr.com
Web: www.franklinstreetfurniture.com

Craig Johnson
Studio Tupla
PO Box 131811
Saint Paul, MN 55113-0020
Email: craig@studiotupla.com
Web: www.studiotupla.com

Randy Johnson
Email: randy.johnson@shopbottools.com

Simon Johnson
516 Briar Rd.
Bellingham, WA 98225
Email: j@pomgrp.com

April Jones
April Jones Studio
900 King St.
Apt 17-A
Charleston, SC 29403
Email: april.apl@gmail.com
Web: www.apriljonesstudio.com

Douglas Jones
Email: randomorbitstudio@hotmail.com

Gary Jonland
Web: www.garyjonland.com

Marge Kaczala
109 State St.
Newburyport, MA 01950
Email: makaczala@comcast.net

Danny Kamerath
677 Upper Turtle Creek Rd.
Kerrville, TX 78028
Email: danny@dannykamerath.com
Web: www.dannykamerath.com

Max Kaplan
MacsaiKaplan
19300 North Corry St.
Fort Bragg, CA 95437
Email: mmacsai@gmail.com
Web: www.macsaikaplan.com/

Peter Kasper
3411 Ivy Ave Sw
Tiffin, IA 52340
Email: peterkasperwoodworks@gmail.com
Web: www.facebook.com/lumberjock89

Clark Kellogg
2303-B Dunlavy
Houston, TX 77006
Email: clark@kelloggfurniture.com
Web: www.kelloggfurniture.com

David Kellum
Email: david52@olympus.net

John Kelsey
2148 Landis Valley Rd.
Lancaster, PA 17601
Email: editorkelsey@gmail.com

Christopher Kemler
2729 Oak Trail
Carrollton, TX 75007
Email: chriskemler@gmail.com
Web: chriskemler.tumblr.com

James Kennell
Email: jlkennell@comcast.net

Justin Kindelspire
89 Church St.
Minneapolis, MN 55455
Email: kinde035@umn.edu

Justin & Paula King
Rexhill Furniture
20 N. Brett St.
Beacon, NY 12508
Email: info@rexhillfurniture.com
Web: www.rexhillfurniture.com

John Kirschenbaum
6555 5th Avenue South #212
Seattle, WA 98108
Email: jnkbaum@gmail.com

Greg Klassen
PO Box 415
Lyndon, WA 98264-0415
Email: furnitureorganic@hotmail.com

Greg Klassen
Email: greg@gregklassen.com

Charles Kline
340 Hammond St.
Chestnut Hill, MA 02467
Email: charlie@theklines.org

Marie Kline
230 Madison St.
Oakland, CA 94607
Email: mariekline@earthlink.net

David Knobel
4826 17th Ave NW
Olympia, WA 98502
Email: dlknobel@comcast.net

David Knopp
6609 Sherwood Rd.
Baltimore, MD 21239
Email: dlknopp@verizon.net

Roger Knudson
RWK Furniture
PO Box 264
Finlayson, MN 55735
Email: rwknudson@frontiernet.net

Charlie Kocourek
Ruby Woodworking & Design
6330 Arthur St. NE
Fridley, MN 55432
Email: charlie@jack-bench.com
Web: www.jack-bench.com

Liz Koerner
39 Hanover St.
Asheville, NC 28806
Email: liz.koerner@gmail.com
Web: www.liz-koerner.com

Mark Koons
407 11th St.
Wheatland, Wyoming 82201
Email: mark@markkoons.com

Silas Kopf
Kopf Woodworking
20 Stearns Ct.
Northampton, MA 01060
Email: silas@silaskopf.com

Sam Kott
130 Cook Lane
Marlboro, MA 01752
Email: sk1491@comcast.net

Janine Kottmyer
4101 W. 98th St., Apt. 226
Bloomington, MN 55437
Email: jkottmye@gmail.com
Web: www.cargocollective.com/
kottmyerconceptualcrafts

Joel Krakauer
623 15th St.
Bellingham, WA 98225
Email: joelkrakauer@gmail.com

Marty Kremer
Email: mail@kremerglass.com

John Kriegshauser
1058 W. 34th Place
Chicago, IL 60608
Email: kriegshauser@iit.edu

Charles Krueger
526 Summit Ave.
Westfield, NJ 07090
Email: porch4@aol.com

Chris Kubash
12408 - 49 Ave NW
Edmonton, AB T6H 0H2
Canada
Email: ckubash@gmail.com
Web: www.kubashstudiofurniture.com

Kyle Kulchar
662 Lake Drive SE
Grand Rapids, MI 49503-4446
Email: Kulchak@ferris.edu

Deborah Kwoh
2404 Jacaranda Ave.
Carlsbad, CA 92009-9111
Email: dykwoh@sbcglobal.net

Sam Ladwig
3015 N. RobinsonAve.
Oklahoma City, OK 73103
Email: srladwig@gmail.com
Web: www.samladwig.com

Tai Lake
Tai Lake Fine Woodwork
PO Box 584
Holualoa, HI 96725
Email: tailake@msn.com

Augustus Lammers
199 Joseph St.
East Brunswick, NJ 08816
Email: info@alammersfurniture.com
Web: www.alammersfurniture.com/

Laura Langelüddecke
Email: llangelueddecke@gmail.com

Aleya Lanteigne
Email: amlantei@umail.iu.edu

Don Laporte
61 CharlrodAve.
Somerset, MA 02726-4716
Email: don.laporte@gmail.com

John Lavine
Westmoor High School
2434 9th St.
Berkeley, CA 94710
Email: johnclavine@gmail.com

Roch Laviolette
Roch Laviolette Studio
PO Box 358
5 Rideau St.
Westport, ON K0G 1X0
Canada
Email: laviolet@rideau.net

Christine Lee
2833 Windstone Glen
Escondido, CA 92027
Email: missleelee33@yahoo.com

Paul Legere
5542 First Line RR3
Acton, ON L7J 2L9
Canada
Email: p.legere@ymail.com

Carol Lemke
JCL Enterprise Inc.
PO Box 529
Livermore, CA 94551
Email: carol@jcl-inc.com

Po Shun Leong
Po Shun Leong Studio
8546 OsoAve.
Winnetka, CA 91306-1341
Email: poshunl@gmail.com
Web: www.poshunleong.com/

Peter Leue
19 Golder St.
Albany, NY 12209
Email: peterleuedesignercraftsman@gmail.com

Mark Levin
125 Mountain Park Place NW, Ste. D
Albuquerque, NM 87114-2222
Email: markslevin@yahoo.com
Web: www.marklevin.com

Aaron Levine
9954 NE Point View Dr.
Bainbridge Island, WA 98110
Email: aaron@aaronlevine.net
Web: www.aaronlevine.net

Aled Lewis
Email: aled@aledlewisfurniture.com
Web: www.aledlewisfurniture.com

Chen Li
c/o San Francisco WoodShop
3450 3rd St. # 5E
San Francisco, CA 94124
Web: www.sanfranciscowoodshop.com/chen-li

Wayne Liang
95 Holden St.
Providence, RI 02903
Email: wliang@risd.edu

Zackary Tyler Lindemann
2145 Ebers St.
San Diego, CA 92107
Email: zlindemann13@gmail.com

Rex Lingwood
925924 Con. 13, R.R.#1
Bright, ON N0J 1B0
Canada
Email: rex@rexlingwood.ca

Gregg Lipton
3 Mill Ridge Rd.
Cumberland, ME 04021
Email: gregg@liptonfurniture.com
Web: www.liptonfurniture.com/

Chris Littlefield
110 Whitford St.
Warwick, RI 02889
Email: chris@littlefieldfinewoodworking.com
Web: www.littlefieldfinewoodworking.com/

Calen Liverance
528 DetroitAve.
Iron Mountain, MI 49801
Email: cjliverance@gmail.com

Rick Lloyd
1890 Skylark Place
Victoria, BC V8N 2X1
Canada
Email: ricklloyd@telus.net

Tally Locke
816 SE Peacock Ln.
Portland, OR 97214
Email: tallylocke@gmail.com

Wayne Locke
Locke Design & Woodworks
9000 Feather Hill Rd.
Austin, TX 78737
Email: wayne@lockedesign.net
Web: www.lockedesign.net

Thomas Loeser
2826 LakelandAve.
Madison, WI 53704
Email: tloeser@wisc.edu

Ted Lott
PO Box 191
Ephraim, WI 54211
Email: ted@tedlott.com
Web: www.tedlott.com/home.html

Brett Lundy
251 Sorauren Ave., Suite 401
Toronto, ON M6R 2G3
Canada
Email: info@merganzer.com
Web: www.merganzer.com

James Macdonald
17 Meadow Lane
Burnham, ME 04922
Email: jmacs@uninets.net
Web: www.jmacwooddesign.com

Coral Mallow
132 Deane St. #3
New Bedford, MA 02746
Email: cmallow@umassd.edu

Chris Mann
Mann Designs
715 S. 22nd St.
Arlington, VA 22202
Email: chris@manndesigns.com
Web: www.manndesigns.com

John Marckworth
535 Cass St.
Port Townsend, WA 98368
Email: john@marckworthdesign.com
Web: www.marckworthdesign.com

Josh Markel
Philadephia Invitational Furniture Show
3605 Hamilton St.
Philadelphia, PA 19104-2327
Email: info@pffshow.com

Sarah Marriage
Sarah Marriage Furniture
1010 WillowAve.
Suite 4
Hoboken, NJ 07030
Email: semarr@semarr.com

Bob Marsh
1180 Gettysburg Pike
Dillsburg, PA 17019
Email: bobmarsh5@juno.com

Gay and Chuck Marshall
32 Wistar Rd.
Paoli, PA 19301-1838
Email: cgmarshall@nni.com

Kerry Marshall
10951 Gurley Ln.
Mendocino, CA 95460
Email: marshall@mcn.org
Web: www.kmwoodworking.net

Chris Martin
1512 FloridaAve.
Ames, IA 50014
Email: chmartin@iastate.edu
Web: www.chrismartinfurniture.com/

Sarah Martin
1502 Mildred Dr.
Murray, KY 42071
Email: slmarti22@gmail.com

Jarrett Maxwell
Email: j.a.max7@gmail.com

Karen McBride
3133 Woodkilton Rd.
Dunrobin, ON K0A 1T0
Canada
Email: kmcsmart@gmail.com
Web: www.woodkiltonstudio.com/

Tim McCarthy
1020 N. Normandie
Los Angeles, CA 90029
Email: crayola96@gmail.com

Paul McClelland
11135 Southwest 78th Court
11135 Southwest 78th Court
Miami, FL 33156
Email: pem@pmcustom.com
Web: www.pmcustom.com

Jerry McEvoy
1575 Mountain St. West
Fruitvale, BC V0G1L1
Canada
Email: jerry@finewoodgallery.com
Web: www.finewoodgallery.com

Tom McFadden
Tom McFadden Furniture
13750 Highway 128
Boonville, CA 95415
Email: tamcfad@pacific.net
Web: www.mcfaddenfurniture.com

Scott McGlasson
Email: scott@woodsport.net

Sean Mckenzie
Web: www.mckenziegallery.com

Geoffrey McKonly
Geoff McKonly Custom Woodworking
28 WoodbineAve.
Northampton, MA 01060
Email: geoffmckonly@gmail.com
Web: www.geoffmckonly.com/

Alison McLennan
AJM Furniture
5533 Broadway
Oakland, CA 94618
Email: ajmfurniture@gmail.com
Web: www.ajm-furniture.com

Kimberly McNeelan
1100 Olema-Bolinas Rd.
Bolinas, CA 94924-9615
Email: kmcneelan@gmail.com

Gordon Meacham
1247 Quince St.
San Mateo, CA 94402
Email: gmeasmca@aol.com

Mark Meier
3636 Meadow Grove Trail
Ann Arbor, MI 48108-9317
Email: Markmeier@comcast.net
Web: www.mkmra2.blogspot.com/

James Mellick
Heartwood Studios and Farm
15040 Maple Ridge Rd.
Milford Center, OH 43045
Email: jmellick@embarqmail.com
Web: www.jamesmellick.com

Lauryn Menard
Email: laurynmenard7@gmail.com

Brian Messenger
Email: brianmessenger@gmail.com

Annie Meyer
2 Walker Terrace
Cambridge, MA 02138
Email: anniemeyerstudio@gmail.com
Web: www.anniemeyerstudio.com

Allen Miesner
Miesner Design
431 Irwin St
San Rafael, CA 94901
Email: info@miesner.com
Web: www.miesner.com

Rob Millard-Mendez
1721 Bayard Park Dr.
Evansville, IN 47714
Email: robmillard2@hotmail.com
Web: www.robmillardmendez.com

Lon Miller
1504 W. MountainAve.
Fort Collins, CO 80521
Email: lonmiller@aol.com

Stephanie Miller
1965 Damen St.
Moscow, ID 83843
Email: stmiller@uidaho.edu

Melissa Miralles
355 Oxford Dr.
Port Moody, BC V3H 1T1
Canada
Email: melubee@hotmail.com

Charles Mitchell
Mitchell Studios
643 Olympic Hot Springs Rd.
Port Angeles, WA 98363
Email: artistmitchell@me.com

Hugh Montgomery
7869 Fletcher Bay Rd. NE
Bainbridge Island, WA 98110
Email: info@hughmontgomery.com

Michael Moore
O'Doherty Moore Woodworking & Design
41 Birch Meadow Rd.
Merrimac, MA 01860-1826
Email: michael@odohertymoore.com

Doug Moran
Creekside Originals
112 Par 3 Dr.
Millersburg, PA 17061
Email: DJMOriginals@gmail.com
Web: www.CreeksideOriginals.com

Jason Morrison
Morrison Handmade
928 Sanders St.
Indianapolis, IN 46203
Email: Jaybmorrison@comcast.net

Rangeley Morton
15 Danforth Lane
Chelmsford, MA 01824
Email: rangemorton@gmail.com
Web: www.rangeleymorton.com/

Dan Mosheim
PO Box 442
Dorset, VT 05251
Email: dan@dorsetcustomfurniture.com

Travis Mullins
223 Magothy Rd.
Pasadena, MD 21122
Email: tmullinsfurniture@gmail.com

David Munkittrick
1108 Town Hall Rd.
River Falls, WI 54022
Email: dmunkit@me.com

Lionel Murphy
9527 Granite Farm Rd.
Sandy, UT 84092
Email: lionelbmurphy@gmail.com

Matthew Nafranowicz
2033 AtwoodAve.
Madison, WI 53704
Email: matthew@thestraightthread.com
Web: www.thestraightthread.com

Cory Nalbone
Email: photobones@gmail.com

Eric Nation
152 N. Main St.
Morrill, ME 04952
Email: eric@ericnation.com
Web: www.ericnation.com

Brad Reed Nelson
Email: bradreednelson@gmail.com

Mya Nelson
2642 39th Street NW
Washington, DC 20007
Email: myarae@gmail.com

Joseph Nemeth
320 W. Oak St.
Ramsey, NJ 07446
Email: joseph@tempestwoodworking.com
Web: www.tempestfurniture.com

Dave Newbold
Email: dave@dnewbold.com

Jan Nielsen
West Wind Hardwood Inc.
PO Box 2205
5-10189 McDonald Park Rd.
Sidney, BC V8L 5X5
Canada
Email: shelley@westwindhardwood.com
Web: www.westwindhardwood.com

Karl Nielsen
Nielsen Fine Woodworking
1119 Cheleek Rd.
Oak Harbor, WA 98277
Email: nielsenoak@hotmail.com

Bart Niswonger
481 Kinnebrook Rd.
Worthington, MA 01098
Email: web@bartniswonger.com
Web: www.bartniswonger.com

Craig Nutt
Craig Nutt Fine Wood Works
1305 Kingston Springs Rd.
Kingston Springs, TN 37082
Email: cn@craignutt.com
Web: www.craignutt.com

Francis O'Brien
411 Walnut St.
Harrisburg, PA 17101
Email: fran@liquorlaw.com

Terry O'Donnell
323 Vincent Dr.
Mountain View, CA 94041-2211
Email: terryeod@gmail.com

Ian O'Hare
8521 Rosedale Dr.
Oak Ridge, NC 27310
Email: iantohare@gmail.com

Christy Oates
9117 Gaucho Ln
El Cajon, CA 92021
Email: info@christyoatesdesign.com
Web: www.christyoates.com

Jeffrey Ochsner
University of Washington
13226 42nd Avenue NE
Seattle, WA 98125
Email: jochsner@uw.edu

Richard Oedel
Fort Point Cabinetmakers
25 Drydock Ave., 2nd floor
Boston, MA 02210
Email: roedel@finefurnituremaster.com
Web: www.finefurnituremaster.com

James Oleson
1421 Gray Bluff Trail
Chapel Hill, NC 27517
Email: jncoleson@bellsouth.net
Web: www.jro-furnituremaker.com

Clarke Olsen
373 Route 203
Spencertown, NY 12165
Email: colsen@taconic.net
Web: www.clarkeolsen.com

Katherine Ortega-Ford
5179 Diane Lane
Livermore, CA 94550
Email: kortegafurniture@gmail.com

Matthew Osborn
820 N HamiltonAve.
Indianapolis, IN 46201
Email: osborndesignandcraft@gmail.com
Web: www.osborndesignandcraft.com/

Benjamin Osborne
221 Dogwood Lake Trail
Alpharetta, GA 30004
Email: benjie@thiswasatree.com
Web: www.thiswasatree.com

Todd Ouwehand
PO Box 661963
Los Angeles, CA 90066-8763
Email: toddman57@aol.com
Web: www.toddouwehand.com

Marcus Papay
1098 HygeiaAve.
San Diego, CA 92024
Email: marcesemo@gmail.com
Web: www.papaydesigns.com

Allan Parachini
Allan Parachini Custom Furniture
2319 Kamali'i St.
Kilauea, HI 96754
Email: aparachini@parachinigroup.com

Clinton Parker
4021 woodland
Royal Oak, MI 48073
Email: thewoodlandstudio@gmail.com

Kelly Parker
12315 NW 66th St.
Parkville, MO 64152
Email: kelly@woodsongstudio.com
Web: www.woodsongstudio.com

Tahle Patton
7712 18th Ave NE
Seattle, WA 98115
Email: tpatton@teleport.com

Richard Peirce
158 Greenmeadow Drive
Timonium, MD 21093
Email: peirce.rk@gmail.com

John A Pennisi, Jr.
Email: john@pennisifinefurniture.com

Jay Perrine
891 Almarida Drive
Campbell, CA 95008
Email: perrinedazign@gmail.com

Peter Pestalozzi
1568 McMahan Blvd
Ely, MN 55731
Email: odysseydesign@hotmail.com
Web: www.odysseydesignworks.com

Myrl Phelps
76 Ragged Mountain Rd.
Danbury, NH 03230
Email: myrlp@yahoo.com

Michael Pietragalla
Floating Stone Woodworks
88 Hatch
Loft 406
Fairhaven, MA 02745
Email: floatingstone@comcast.net

Kurt Piper
34 Front St.
Building 2, 5th Floor
Indian Orchard, MA 01151
Email: info@piperwoodworking.com
Web: www.piperwoodworking.com

Norman Pirollo
Pirollo Design
8226 Rodney Farm Drive
Ottawa, ON K0A 2P0
Canada
Email: studio@refinededge.com
Web: www.pirollodesign.com

Andrew Pitts
Andrew Pitts - FurnitureMaker
667 Courthouse Rd.
Heathsville, VA 22473
Email: workshop@andrewpittsfurnituremaker.com
Web: www.AndrewPittsFurnitureMaker.com

Leslie Podell
3966 Washington St.
San Francisco, CA 94118
Email: lpodell@cca.edu

Michael Podmaniczky
1715 North Rodney St.
Wilmington, DE 19806
Email: mikepod44@gmail.com

Christopher Poehlmann
CP Lighting
3201 Fox St.
Philadelphia, PA 19129
Email: chris@cplighting.com
Web: www.cplighting.com

Margaret Polcawich
7508 Nutwood Court
Derwood, MD 20855-2232
Email: margaret@handsculptedfurniture.com

Charlie Price
6089 CerritosAve.
Long Beach, CA 90805
Email: price90806@yahoo.com

Garth Priest
1010 Princess Anne St.
Fredericksburg, VA 22401
Email: garthpriest@gmail.com

Richard Prisco
892 Windwood Lane
Boone, NC 28607
Email: art4mz@gmail.com
Web: www.richardprisco.com/home.html

Dean Pulver
PO Box 1457
El Prado, NM 87529
Email: dean@deanpulver.com
Web: www.deanpulver.com

Michael Puryear
Michael Puryear Furnituremaker
46 Longyear Rd.
Shokan, NC 12481
Email: mpuryear@pipeline.com
Web: www.michaelpuryear.com

Brian Quan
140 Kings Highway
Boulder Creek, CA 95006
Email: bquan@ucsc.edu

Charles Radtke
W62 N732 Riveredge Drive
Cedarburg, WI 53012
Email: charlesradtke@charlesradtke.com

Mike Randall
Kurva Design
1417 Pembroke St.
Victoria, BC V8R 1V7
Canada
Email: mike@kurvadesign.ca
Web: www.kurvadesign.ca

David Rasmussen
345 ColoradoAve.
Suite 207
Carbondale, CO 81623
Email: David@davidrasmussendesign.com

Martin Ratermann
1136 Highway 40
New Franklin, MO 65274
Email: martin@martinratermann.com

Andrew Redington
University of Wisconsin Oshkosh–Art Dept.
800 Algoma Buleva Rd.
Oshkosh, WI 54901
Email: redingto@uwosh.edu

Paul Reiber
44051 Fern Creek Rd.
Caspar, CA 95420
Email: preiber@mcn.org
Web: www.mendocinofurniture.com/artists/17

Molly Reynolds
12513 W 101st Place
St John, IN 46373
Email: molereyno@gmail.com

Michael Reznikoff
328 Thomas Place
Everman, TX 76140
Email: mike@reznikoff.net

Justin Richards
2038 Camp St.
New Orleans, LA 70130
Email: justin@justinbuilds.com
Web: www.justinbuilds.com

Chris Rifkin
16 Causeway Rd.
Hingham, MA 02043
Email: chris4013@comcast.net

Jose R. Riveros
Email: jose.riveros666@gmail.com

Jodi Robbins
Email: jodi@halfcrowndesign.com

Lauren Robillard
9028 Tenton Court
Indianapolis, IN 46278
Email: laurobil@umail.iu.edu

Cory Robinson
Robinson Studio
4148 Vera Dr.
Indianapolis, IN 46220
Email: cordrobi@iupui.edu
Web: www.coryrobinsonstudio.com

Gerald Robson
Gerald Robson Engineering
2120 Wenman Dr.
Victoria, BC V8N 2S2
Canada
Email: garobson@shaw.ca

Kevin Rodel
Kevin Rodel Furniture & Design Studio
14 Maine St.
Brunswick, ME 04011
Email: kevin@kevinrodel.com
Web: www.kevinrodel.com

Jo Roessler
84 Cottage St.
Easthampton, MA 01027
Email: info@nojodesign.com

Seth Rolland
Seth Rolland Custom Furniture
1039 Jackson St.
Port Towsend, WA 98368-4509
Email: seth@olypen.com
Web: www.sethrolland.com

Gabriel Romeu
315 Crosswicks Ellisdale
Chesterfield, NJ 08515
Email: romeug@live.com

Fred Rose
Email: fredrosestudio@yahoo.com

Jim Rose
Email: jim@jimrosefurniture.com

Nathan Rose
Rose Woodworks
6325 W. Wilkinson Blvd., Ste. D
Belmont, NC 28012
Email: nathanrose@carolina.rr.com

Jason Rossitto
Email: jasongetsdown@gmail.com

Hunter Roth
Web: www.hunterroth.com

Phil Rowland
4305 Corinth St.
San Diego, CA 92115
Email: phil.rowland@gmail.com

Rejean Roy
271 des Vosges
St-Lambert, QC J4S 1M1
Canada
Email: rejean-roy@videotron.ca

M. Carol Salvin
6612 Gunn Dr.
Oakland, CA 94611
Email: carol@mcarol.com
Web: www.mcarol.com

Peter Sandoval
5311 Joe Wilson Rd.
Midlothian, TX 76065
Email: Peter@carpentryassociates.com

Benjamin Saperstein
Email: bsaperstein@cca.edu

Fabiano Sarra
Anderson Ranch Arts Center
5263 Owl Creek Rd.
PO Box 5598
Snowmass Village, CO 81615
Email: fabianosarra@gmail.com

J. Sassaman
Autodesk
Pier 9, the Embarcadero
Autodesk Bay #C
San Francisco, CA 94111
Email: j.sassaman@autodesk.com

Maggie Sasso
1636 E Eden Pl
Saint Francis, WI 53235
Email: maggiesasso@gmail.com
Web: www.maggiesasso.com

Jeffrey Scanlan
805 Marguerite Rd.
Metairie, LA 70003
Email: jeffreyscanlan@hotmail.com

Bill Schairer
4565 Alice St.
San Diego, CA 92115
Email: billschairer@me.com

Jeff Schauer
125 Lewis Rd.
Belmont, MA 02478
Email: jeffro@ameritech.net

Peter Scheidt
Email: peter.n.scheidt@gmail.com

Jamie Schell
Email: jamie@jamieschell.com

Jeff Schrader
20531 Philadelphia Way
Eagle River, Alaska 99577
Email: jeff.schrader@bp.com

Anelise Schroeder
10 Bowen Street #3E
Providence, RI 02903
Email: aschroed@risd.edu

Bruce Schuettinger
Art in Furniture by Schuettinger
P.O. Box 244
New Market, MD 21774
Email: bschuettinger@verizon.net
Web: www.artinfurniture.com

Ian Schwandt
215 N Mabbettsville Rd.
Millbrook, NY 12545
Email: ianschwandt@gmail.com
Web: www.ijswoodworking.com

Jay T Scott
Jay T Scott Woodworking
505 Flora Vista Rd. NE
Olympia, WA 98506
Email: jayt@jaytscott.com
Web: www.jaytscott.com

Kelly Scott
3716 Canon Gate Circle
Carrollton, TX 75007
Email: kelly_scott@verizon.net

Adrien Segal
Email: adriensegal@gmail.com

Wyatt Severs
905 Olive St.
Murray, KY 42071
Email: wyattsevers@gmail.com
Web: www.wyattsevers.com

Chuck Sharbaugh
14039 Candlewick Drive
Holly, MI 48442-9505
Email: csharbaugh@comcast.net
Web: www.chucksharbaugh.com

Alf Sharp
3130 Doolittle Rd.
Woodbury, TN 37190
Email: asharp@dtccom.net

Tory Sharples
4184 Clinton Place
Victoria, BC V8Z 6M1
Canada
Email: trsharples@hotmail.com

Cameron Shaw
411 14th Ave. E
Seattle, WA 98112
Email: csshaw89@gmail.com

Liz Sheehan
9 Bedford Drive
Doylestown, PA 18902
Email: lizksheehan@gmail.com
Web: www.lizksheehan@gmail.com

John Sheridan
3450 Third St., #5-E.
San Francisco, CA 94124-1439
Email: grew_sheridan@mac.com

Tom Shields
81 AnnandaleAve.
Asheville, NC 28801
Email: xtomshieldsx@gmail.com

Jay Siegelaub
246 Woods Brooke Circle
Ossining, NY 10562
Email: jms@sibat.net

Susie Silbert
256 5thAve.
Apt. 4F
Brooklyn, NY 11215
Email: sjsilbert@gmail.com

Dustin Sims
205 Bretonshire Rd.
Wilmington, NC 28405
Email: simsd510@gmail.com

Michael Singer
1170 El Solyo Heights Dr.
Felton, CA 95018
Email: mms@msfinewoodworking.com
Web: www.msfinewoodworking.com

Brandon Skupski
64 Bradley St.
Asheville, NC 28806
Email: ironandashfurniture@gmail.com
Web: www.ironandashfurniture.com

Janice Smith
715 S. 7th St.
Philadelphia, PA 19147
Email: not2wooden@earthlink.net

Joshua Smith
Smith Workshop
560 N Corry St.
Fort Bragg, CA 95437
Email: smithwkshp@gmail.com
Web: www.smith-workshop.com

Scott Smith
310 Jefferson Dr.
Pittsburgh, PA 15228
Email: ssbg@andrew.cmu.edu

Stephanie Smith
4330 Houlihan Pl
Victoria, BC V8N 3T1
Canada
Email: stefynsmith@gmail.com

Maryah Smith-Overman
Box 38
Shiloh, NJ 08353
Email: ryaolive@yahoo.com

Freeland Southard
244 Harbor Ridge Ln.
Kokomo, IN 46901, OH 44077
Email: superfreeland@yahoo.com
Web: www.superfreeland.com/home.html

Jerry Spady
108 E. Geneva Ln.
Oak Ridge, TN 37830
Email: jerry@jerry.com

Fred Spencer
2105 Constance Dr.
Oakville, Ontario L6J 5V1
Canada
Email: fred.spencer@cogeco.ca

Dolly Spragins
Dolly Spragins, Art.Furniture
1909 Francisco St.
Berkeley, CA 94709
Email: comets@comcast.net
Web: www.dollyspragins.com

Worth Squire
PO Box 248
College Grove, TN 37046-0248
Email: worths@united.net

Jay Stanger
390 Center St.
P.O. Box 494
South Easton, MA 02375
Email: Jay@jaystanger.com

Jacob Stanley
Email: jacob.k.stanley@gmail.com

Todd Steffy
615 West Zwilling Rd.
Erie, PA 16509
Email: TLSteffy@hotmail.com

Richard Steinberg
101 Banyan Isle Dr.
Palm Beach Gardens, FL 33418
Email: richard3979@gmail.com

Walter Stevens
497 Route 55
Eldred, NY 12732
Email: bo.wswd@gmail.com

Scott Stewart
Scott Stewart Designs
4701 SE 24th Ave., #W2
Portland, OR 97202
Email: scott@scottstewartdesigns.com
Web: www.scottstewartdesigns.com/

Allen Stone
5235 West RowlandAve.
Littleton, CO 80128
Email: astone@stoneswood.com
Web: www.stoneswood.com

Doug Stowe
Douglas Stowe, Inc.
412 Sandrock Rd.
PO Box 247
Eureka Springs, AR 72632-0247
Email: dstowe@arkansas.net
Web: www.wisdomofhands.blogspot.com

Tucker Strasser
505 BoccaccioAve.
Venice, CA 90291
Email: rtswoodworking@gmail.com

David Strauss
David Strauss Designs
14 Grayson Lane
Newton, MA 02462
Email: davidstraussdesigns@outlook.com
Web: www.davidstraussdesigns.com

Clinton (Clint) Struthers
304 W. Wackerly St.
Midland, MI 48640
Email: clint@sorraiastudios.com

Robert Sukrachand
308 OnderdonkAve.
Ridgewood, NY 11385
Email: robertsukrachand@gmail.com

Sam Takahashi
6465 EdmontonAve.
San Diego, CA 92122
Email: stakahashi@yahoo.com

Arthur Talayko
Email: arthurtalayko@gmail.com

Derek Taylor
Email: taylor.hamiltond@gmail.com

Abraham Tesser
308 West Lake Dr.
Athens, GA 30606
Email: atesser@tesserfurniture.com
Web: www.tesserfurniture.com

John Thayer
100 Lagoon Pond Rd.
Vineyard Haven, MA 02568
Email: john@johnthayer.com
Web: www.johnthayer.com

Robert Then
Email: artmetal@att.net

Charles Thomas
5893 S Sherman Way
Centennial, CO 80121
Email: charles@thomasbrothersworkshop.com

James Thomas
PO Box 957
Niwot, CO 80544
Email: jimt1953@gmail.com

Elizabeth Thorp
174 Butterfield Rd.
San Anselmo, CA 94960
Email: eliz.thorp@gmail.com
Web: www.elizabeththorp.com

Thomas Throop
26 Grove St.
New Canaan, CT 06840-5323
Email: tom@blackcreekdesigns.com
Web: www.blackcreekdesigns.com

Megan Tilston
50 Fifth St.
Toronto, ON M8V 2Z2
Canada
Email: megan.tilston@primus.ca

Joshua Torbick
4150 Texas St., #7
San Diego, CA 92104
Email: jtorbick@gmail.com
Web: www.joshuatorbickfurniture.com/

Allen Townsend
12 Durham Dr.
Andover, MA 01810
Email: allenltownsend@outlook.com

Heater Trautlinde
P.O. Box V V
Aspen, CO 81612
Email: trautheater@aol.com

Paul Troyano
Living Furniture
4738 Palmyra St.
New Orleans, LA 70119
Email: pjt@livingfurniture.net
Web: www.livingfurniture.net

John Tucker
3544 SavannahAve.
Victoria, BC V8X 1S5
Canada
Email: jetucker51@yahoo.ca

Michael Tudor
2041 Anna Dr.
Elkhart, IN 46514-3126
Email: tudorhome@frontier.com

Colin Tury
5220 Oak Leaf Dr. Apt. A2
Indianapolis, IN 46220
Email: colin.tury@gmail.com

Anita Tyiska
Padouk Furniture+Design
2901 16th St. NW #403
Washington, DC
Washington, DC, DC 20009
Email: actyiska@gmail.com

Josh Urso
Josh Urso Design
347 Varick St.
Suite 316A
Jersey City, NJ 07302
Email: josh@joshursodesign.com
Web: www.joshursodesign.com

Nicholas Van Gorp
Email: nichvang@gmail.com
Web: www.nvangorp-mcad.blogspot.com

Hannah Vaughan
Email: hannah.vaughan@gmail.com

Bob Vergette
1103 Walden Rd., RR#1
Pender Island, BC V0N 2M1
Canada
Email: bvergette@shaw.ca

Kerry Vesper
Vesper Sculpture and Design, LLC
116 E. Ellis Dr.
Tempe, AZ 85282
Email: kerry@kerryvesper.com
Web: www.kerryvesper.com

Derrick Vocelka
2433 Apache Dr
Bishop, CA 93514
Email: dvocelka@cebridge.net

Adam Vorrath
7695 Forestay Dr
Lake Worth, FL 33467
Email: adamvorrath@gmail.com

Laura Wagner
7401 Liz Ct
Los Angeles, CA 91304
Email: hazelnutt1@aol.com

Daniel Waldburger
7948 Roseland Dr
La Jolla, CA 92037
Email: danwal58@gmail.com

Barbara Waldman
San Fancisco, CA
Email: barbarawaldman@mac.com

William Walker
Email: wmbwalker@q.com

Paulus Wanrooij
708 Harpswell Neck Rd.
Harpswell, ME 04079
Email: paulus@paulusfurniture.com

Jordan Waraksa
165 W TripoliAve.
Milwaukee, WI 53207
Email: jordanwaraksa@yahoo.com
Web: www.jordanwaraksa.com

Pat Warner
3 Benton St.
Wellesley, MA 02482-6903
Email: thewarners2@verizon.net

Mark Wedekind
2136 Alder Dr.
Anchorage, AK 99508
Web: blackstonedesign.com

Tim Weiss
173 Emerald Bay
Laguna Beach, CA 92651
Email: timweiss@mac.com

David Welter
552 South Harold St.
Fort Bragg, CA 95437
Email: dwelter@mcn.org

Tom Wessells
4 Graham Dr.
Newport News, VA 23606
Email: tommot22@aol.com
Web: www.furniturebytom.com

Brian Westra
2875 Cheryl St.
Eugene, OR 97408
Email: bdwestra24@yahoo.com

Steven White
336 Hammond St.
Bishop, CA 93514
Email: steve@stevenwhitewoodworking.com
Web: www.stevenwhitewoodworking.com

Mark Whitley
1711 Patterson Rd.
Smith's Grove, KY 42171
Web: www.mwhitely.com

Kevin Wiggers
Wiggers Furniture
Beaverton, Ontario L0K1A0
Canada
Email: kevinwiggers@wiggersfurniture.com
Web: www.wiggersfurniture.com

John Williams
HC 68 Box 18GG
Renick, WV 24966
Email: jwilliams5@earthlink.net

Johnny Williams
Email: johnnyawilliams@gmail.com

Eric Wilmot
Email: eric@ericwilmot.fr

Fo Wilson
1906 South Halsted St.
Unit # 1 Rear
Chicago, IL 60608
Email: fo@fowilson.com

Kimberly Winkle
1862 Puckett Point Rd.
Smithville, TN 37166
Email: wimkinkle@yahoo.com
Web: www.kimberlywinkle.com

Erik Wolken
Works in Wood
127 Ladybug Lane
Chapel Hill, NC 27516
Email: erik@erikwolken.com
Web: www.erikwolken.com

Ted Wong
350 E. Spring St.
Oxford, OH 45056
Email: wongtw@miamioh.edu

Stewart Wurtz
Stewart Wurtz Furniture
3410 Woodland Park Ave. N
Seattle, WA 98103
Email: stewart@stewartwurtz.com

Nico Yektai
290 Widow Gavits Rd.
PO Box 1088
Sag Harbor, NY 11963
Web: www.nicotektai.com

Takahiro Yoshino
Email: info@tak-yoshino.jp
Web: www.tak-yoshino.jp/en

Stephen Yusko
1487 GraceAve.
Lakewood, OH 44107
Email: syusko@sbcglobal.net
Web: www.stephenyusko.com

Jiri Zapletal
9037 NE 143rd St.
Kirkland, WA 98034
Email: Margaret-Jiri@msn.com

Jingtao Zhang
Email: jzhang@cca.edu

Moyu Zhang
253 River Meadow Dr.
Rochester, NY 14623
Email: vivienmoyuzhang@gmail.com

Hongtao Zhou
3450 Paalea St.
Honolulu, HI 96816
Email: discoverzhou@gmail.com
Web: www.hongtaozhou.com/

Jeremy Zietz
3511 ParkAve.
Apt. 1
Richmond, VA 23221
Email: jeremyzietz@gmail.com
Web: www.jeremyzietzstudio.com

Gregory Znajda
352 HarveyAve.
Des Plaines, IL 60016
Email: gregznajda@gmail.com

NON-PROFIT MEMBERS

Fine Woodworking College of the Redwoods
C/R Fine Woodworking
440 Alger St.
Fort Bragg, CA 95437
Email: woodshop@mcn.org
Web: www.crfinefurniture.com

Haystack Mountain School of Crafts
Stuart Kestenbaum
PO Box 518
Deer Isle, ME 04627-0518
Phone: 207-348-2306
Email: haystack@haystack-mtn.org
Web: www.haystack-mtn.org/

Penland School of Crafts
Dana Moore
PO Box 37
Penland, NC 28765
Phone: 828-765-2359
Email: danamoore@penland.org
Web: www.penland.org/

Rhode Island School of Design
Rhode Island School of Design Furniture Design
2 College St.
Providence, RI 02903
Phone: 401-454-6102
Email: mgrear@risd.edu
Web: www.risd.edu/academics/furniture-design/

University of Idaho
Jay Pengilly
1136 N Mountain View Rd.
University of Idaho
Moscow, ID 83843
Email: pengilly@uidaho.edu
Web: www.uidaho.edu/caa/facilities/tds

AWARD OF DISTINCTION RECIPIENTS

2001
Art Carpenter
Email: artcarpenter@furnituresociety.org

Wendell Castle
18 Maple St.
Scottsville, NY 14546
Email: castlett@aol.com

Tage Frid
Email: tagefrid@furnituresociety.org

James Krenov
Email: jameskrenov@furnituresociety.org

Sam Maloof
Email: sammaloof@furnituresociety.org

2002
John Makepeace
Email: johnmakepeace@furnituresociety.org

Jere Osgood
626 Abbot Hill Rd.
Wilton, NH 03086-9129
Email: jerewood@aol.com

Alan Peters
Email: alanpeters@furnituresociety.org

2003
Jonathan Fairbanks
247 Nahatan St.
Westwood, MA 02090
Email: jleofairbanks@yahoo.com

William Keyser, Jr.
8008 Taylor Rd.
Victor, NY 14564
Email: keywoodart@frontiernet.net

2004
Garry Knox Bennett
130 4th St.
Oakland, CA 94607
Email: gkbfurniture@yahoo.com
Web: gkb-furniture.com

2005
Judy McKie
82 Holworthy St.
Cambridge, MA 02138
Email: judymckie@comcast.net

2006
Tommy Simpson
P.O. Box 2264
New Preston, CT 06777
Email: tommy-simpson@earthlink.net

2007
Michael Fortune
1623 English Line RR #2
Lakefield, ON K0L 2H0
Canada
Email: michael.fortune@sympatico.ca

2008
Wendy Maruyama
4565 Alice St.
San Diego, CA 92115
Email: wendy@wendymaruyama.com
Web: www.wendymaruyama.com

Walker Weed
Email: walkerweed@furnituresociety.org

2009
Vladimir Kagan
1185 Park Ave Apt 14g
New York, NY 10128-1312
Email: vladkagan1@me.com

2010
John Cederquist
Email: johncederquist@furnituresociety.org

2012
Rosanne Somerson
2 College St.
Providence, RI 02903-2784
Email: rs@rsomerson.com

2014
Bebe & Warren Johnson
178 Newtown Lane
East Hampton, NY 11937-2445
Email: connect@pritameames.com